SUPERNATUR...

Get The Scoop

P9-CRD-063

HOLLYWOOD'S
HOTTEST
"IT" GIRLS

Fabulous on the Red Carpet

Starlets with Style

an unauthorized biography about the girls of the Twilight Saga by **JOSI DASHMAN**

PSS!
Price Stern Sloan

MAR 1 0

KN

PRICE STERN SLOAN
Published by the Penguin Group
Penguin Group (USA) Inc., 375 Hudson Street, New York, New York 10014, USA
Penguin Group (Canada), 90 Eglinton Avenue East, Suite 700, Toronto, Ontario M4P 2Y3,
Canada (a division of Pearson Penguin Canada Inc.)
Penguin Books Ltd., 80 Strand, London WC2R 0RL, England
Penguin Group Ireland, 25 St. Stephen's Green, Dublin 2, Ireland
(a division of Penguin Books Ltd.)
Penguin Group (Australia), 250 Camberwell Road, Camberwell, Victoria 3124, Australia (a
division of Pearson Australia Group Pty. Ltd.)
Penguin Books India Pvt. Ltd., 11 Community Centre, Panchsheel Park,
New Delhi—110 017, India
Penguin Group (NZ), 67 Apollo Drive, Rosedale, North Shore 0632, New Zealand
(a division of Pearson New Zealand Ltd.)
Penguin Books (South Africa) (Pty.) Ltd., 24 Sturdee Avenue, Rosebank,
Johannesburg 2196, South Africa

Penguin Books Ltd., Registered Offices: 80 Strand, London WC2R 0RL, England

Photo credits: Cover: Steve Granitz/WireImage; Jon Kopaloff/FilmMagic; Kevin Winter/
Getty Images; Alexandra Wyman/WireImage; Jordan Strauss/WireImage; Insert photos:
first page courtesy of Lester Cohen/WireImage; Kevin Winter/ Getty Images; second page
courtesy of Todd Williamson/WireImage; Jun Sato/WireImage; Lester Cohen/WireImage;
Alberto E. Rodriguez/WireImage; third page courtesy of KMazur/WireImage; Michael
Desmond/Warner Bros.; Todd Williamson/WireImage; Mark Sullivan/WireImage; fourth
page courtesy of Mike Guastella/WireImage; Jordan Strauss/WireImage; Katy Winn/
Getty Images; Todd Williamson/WireImage; fifth page courtesy of Dimitrios Kambouris/
WireImage; Jean Baptiste Lacroix/FilmMagic; Alberto E. Rodriguez/Getty Images; Lester
Cohen/WireImage; sixth page courtesy of Brian To/FilmMagic; Kevin Winter/ Getty Images;
seventh page courtesy of Todd Williamson/WireImage; Chris Polk/FilmMagic; eighth page
courtesy of Charley Gallay/WireImage; Jeff Kravitz/FilmMagic.

Library of Congress Control Number: 2009027538

ISBN 978-0-8431-9953-6   10 9 8 7 6 5 4 3 2 1

CONTENTS

CONTENTS

INTRODUCTION

The crowd of 6,500 fans was ready—and ravenous.

It was July 24, 2008, and the site was Comic-Con in San Diego, California. Comic-Con is a very popular annual convention that was first held at the U.S. Grant Hotel in downtown San Diego in 1970. It began as a meeting place for comic book fanatics, but has grown over the years to showcase movies, TV shows, video games, and other forms of pop culture. Comic-Con specializes in promoting all things supernatural in the entertainment world, so it was the perfect site for what was about to happen.

The massive crowd gathered inside was hungry for a glimpse of the young, superhot actors from the highly anticipated vampire romance movie *Twilight*. The movie is based on the first book in the best-selling series of young adult novels about a life-changing love between seventeen-year-old Bella Swan and Edward Cullen, a vampire who is perpetually seventeen years old. The books had been on the best seller list for some time, but the movie hadn't even come out yet. Still, the fans were clamoring for a look at the actors who were going to bring their favorite book series to life.

According to MTV.com, the crowd stretched for nearly a mile just to get into the *Twilight* cast interview, which featured director Catherine Hardwicke, author Stephenie Meyer, and cast members Kristen Stewart, who plays human protagonist Bella Swan; Robert Pattinson, who plays vampire heartthrob Edward Cullen; Taylor Lautner, who plays Bella's werewolf friend Jacob Black; and Cam Gigandet, Rachelle Lefevre, and Edi Gathegi, who play the film's evil, human-hunting vampire clan.

When the capacity crowd inside the convention center began to chant "*Twilight! Twilight!*" the cast couldn't help but feel nervous. For most of the stars, this was their first big studio movie. And for *all* of the stars, it was the first time they had experienced this kind of hysteria from fans. Amazing, intense, and unbelievable were just some of the words the cast used to try to describe the otherwise indescribable event unfolding before them. In fact, when asked later in interviews to name the first time she realized what a big deal *Twilight* was, the answer was easy for Kristen Stewart: "Comic-Con," she told the *USA Weekend* blog.

When the movie's main stars—Kristen and Robert Pattinson—finally took the stage, the deafening roar of the Twilighters—one of the nicknames given to the incredibly devoted and passionate fans of the book series (they're also called Twihards)—swelled to near-hysteria.

"As you can see, I'm a little nervous," Kristen told the crowd. But the crowd was right there to support the actress who would bring their beloved Bella to life on the big screen. "Don't be nervous, Kristen!" a fan screamed. "We love you!"

The legions of fans continued to cheer and scream, while the actors onstage took in the scene. The crowd only quieted down when an exclusive clip from the movie began to play—that was something they definitely didn't want to miss.

With that level of mayhem, you would think something life-altering was happening inside that packed convention center.

For the female actresses who play the leads in the movie, it already had.

CHAPTER 1
In Her Blood

Kristen Jaymes Stewart was born in Los Angeles on April 9, 1990, to a family that was already pretty familiar with the entertainment industry. Kristen's Australian-born mother, Jules Mann-Stewart, has been a script supervisor in the industry for more than twenty years. A script supervisor is not the same as a screenwriter. Rather, a script supervisor is a member of the film crew who works closely with the director to make sure that a movie's scenes flow properly and that there is consistency with all the film's details. Kristen's father, John Stewart, has been a stage manager, television producer, and director, and his work has been featured extensively on the FOX network. Considering the work that her parents do, it's no surprise that Kristen found a home in showbiz!

Growing up, Kristen had a pretty normal

childhood. She told *Parade* magazine, "I have sort of a picture perfect family. My parents are awesome and my brothers are like my best friends." She was especially close with her older brother, Cameron, who also works in the movie business now as a grip. A grip is a member of a film crew who handles the setup and maintenance of production equipment, such as the cameras and lighting. Kristen has always been so tight with her family, in fact, that she recently told talk show host Jimmy Kimmel on his show *Jimmy Kimmel Live!* that despite her recent fame, she still lives at her family's home in suburban Los Angeles. "I'm really tight with my brothers . . . I just bought a place, but I'm not giving up my bedroom!" she joked.

Kristen is a self-described Valley girl with a love for classic literature and music. "I'm such a home body. I'm pretty boring. I read a lot. I watch a lot of movies. I hang out with my brother," she told moviesonline.ca. You might catch Kristen reading *East of Eden* by John Steinbeck—it's her favorite book.

Kristen also plays guitar, and has for years. But

does she have aspirations for fronting her own band? "I totally wanted to do that when I was little, but [no], I would rather just play with my friends," she told moviesonline.ca. As a kid growing up in California, Kristen was busy learning guitar, but her career would take her in an entirely different direction.

Turns out, Kristen's venture into show business was completely by accident. "It was so weird. It's, like, a very typical L.A. story," she said in an interview on the daytime television talk show *Live with Regis and Kelly.* "I was doing a school play—a very embarrassing Christmas school play—and I was asked to go on auditions."

A talent agent in the audience had been impressed with eight-year-old Kristen's stage presence—she had sung the "Dreidel Song"!—and approached her parents afterward about sending her on auditions.

"My parents were nice enough to actually run it by me . . . instead of just, like, hanging up," she told the *San Francisco Chronicle.* "They [asked me], 'Do you want to do this?' They were not very enthusiastic. They are realistic about the business. It is not a normal thing to be successful at it." It wasn't surprising that the Stewarts were a little hesitant about throwing their young daughter into the cutthroat business they had been working in for years. But, at the same time, their years of experience in Hollywood probably gave them enough insight to know how to protect their daughter, so they finally agreed. Even at that young age, Kristen remembers thinking that it might be cool to go on a few auditions and work on a movie set. It was an environment where she was actually quite comfortable, thanks to her parents' careers. But chances are, little Kristen had no idea at the time the kind of stardom she was in for!

Kristen's first audition was actually more of a "gathering" of child actors that was designed for agents to scout out potential talent. But Kristen wasn't too stressed about it. "I didn't really have anything to be worried about. It wasn't something I needed. It was, like, let's give this a shot. If it hadn't happened, I wouldn't be devastated," she told the *San Francisco Chronicle*. But things have definitely changed since then! "Now if you were to take it away from me, I don't really know what I would do," she continued.

But as luck—or fate—would have it, she nailed her first "audition" and landed an agent, who immediately began booking auditions for film and TV roles.

Even though they were initially reluctant for her to get into show business, Kristen's parents backed her decision to give acting a shot after she got an agent and started landing auditions. But they also made it clear to her that she had the option to quit whenever she wanted to. "[They] don't sit down and give me pointed advice like 'Kristen, you should do this and this,'" she explained to moviesonline.ca. "They've always been really supportive in that [I could] drop out of this at any time [I wanted]. Basically you just have to make yourself happy and you've got to do what you want to do. And they're just really motivating, sort of a driving force, which is something I really need."

Winning roles didn't come overnight, however. Kristen went to her fair share of auditions, but didn't have a lot of luck at first. She was getting really frustrated, and part of her wanted to give up and just go back to life as a normal kid. But Kristen kept working hard, and eventually, she started landing roles! Like most up-and-coming stars, Kristen's earliest work was actually in commercials. A young Kristen appeared in a Porsche commercial as a schoolgirl who intentionally misses the school bus so her father will have to drive her to school in his gorgeous black Porsche. Kristen also snagged bit parts in a couple of the films on which her mother served as script supervisor. She appeared as a girl waiting in line for the drinking fountain in the Disney Channel production called *The Thirteenth Year*. The 1999 made-for-TV movie was about a boy named Cody who turns thirteen and suddenly sprouts fins and scales and starts sparking electricity. A star on the swim team, Cody realizes—with the help of a friend—that he's actually a mer-boy!

Kristen also appeared as the ringtoss girl in *The Flintstones in Viva Rock Vegas*, a live-action film based on the Hanna-Barbera characters and released by Universal Studios in 2000.

When she wasn't going to auditions, Kristen attended a regular school near her home in suburban L.A. until seventh grade. After that, because her career was really picking up, she opted to continue her education through an independent-study program rather than go to a regular junior high or high school. She definitely missed hanging out with her friends between classes and after school, but was glad she had decided to make the switch. "I got so much out of home schooling. I really loved [it]. Independent study is for me," she said of her experience to *Scholastic News*. Plus, Kristen was happy to have avoided a lot of the drama that comes with being a teen in a big high school. She told teenhollywood.com: "I went to school up until . . . the seventh grade, and I know a lot of people who have graduated from high school and everyone gets a major dose of perspective on who their real friends are and what their real values are and what is important to them and that kind of happened for me just a little bit earlier."

For the most part, Kristen's friends are the same ones she had growing up, who have been there for her since her very first audition. "When you're a kid, your friends, your school, your teachers, your family—that's your whole world, your whole existence. And then when I stopped going [to school], I lost all my friends but the few that were really close to me. And I still maintain those friendships," she told *Interview* magazine.

Little did Kristen know that the craziness of her young acting career was headed to a whole new level!

CHAPTER 2
Indie Beginnings

Twilight's large cast was made up of relatively unknown actors. Of the five young *Twilight* actresses, Kristen Stewart had the longest résumé and the most acting experience before *Twilight*. As one of Hollywood's most promising young talents, she had more than twenty movies under her belt before she had even turned nineteen!

The first movie in which she had a speaking role was the 2001 film *The Safety of Objects*. This movie was also significant to Kristen's career in that it was an independent (also known as an "indie" film)— the first of many roles Kristen would eventually play in independent features. Independent features often have smaller budgets and theatrical releases than major motion pictures and feature unknown or up-and-coming actors and actresses, which Kristen definitely was! Kristen excelled in this movie, and the other indies in which she starred. So much so that over the years, she was referred to as a "Sundance 'it' girl"—a reference to the Sundance Film Festival, an annual cinema festival held in Park City, Utah, that showcases the best in American independent films. *The Safety of Objects* was where Kristen first got her start as an indie star!

The Safety of Objects is about four families whose lives become intertwined. Kristen played the character of Sam Jennings, the tomboy daughter of a troubled single mother, who was played by actress Patricia Clarkson. In the movie, Sam is abducted by a disturbed young landscaper when he mistakes her for his younger brother, who died recently. The landscaper is still trying to get over the shock of his brother's accidental death.

Other familiar names in the movie included Glenn Close, Dermot Mulroney, Joshua Jackson, and Moira Kelly. Kristen felt honored to be in the company of such experienced and well-respected actors. Her experience on the set probably cemented her love of working on indie films for the rest of her young acting career!

Kristen loved the experience she got on the set of her first indie, but for up-and-coming actors hungry for more roles, there are few things better than getting a shot to act in a film with a big budget and major stars attached. Kristen got her shot in 2002 when she was cast in a major Hollywood film—the psychological thriller *Panic Room*—with an A-list actress who, like Kristen, had gotten her start acting very young: Jodie Foster. A two-time Academy Award winner for Best Actress in a Leading Role, Jodie started out in television at the age of three and soon added film roles to her résumé. She appeared as a daughter who switches bodies with her mother in the original Disney comedy *Freaky Friday* when she was just a few years older than Kristen.

In *Panic Room*, Kristen played Sarah Altman, the moody and diabetic eleven-year-old daughter of Jodie's character, Meg Altman. Recently divorced and rolling in money from her ex-husband, Meg buys a huge Upper West Side home in Manhattan to help give herself and her daughter a fresh start. The house even includes a "panic room," a specially equipped concrete space designed to keep you safe when burglars invade your home. It contains surveillance monitors and a separate phone line behind a steel door that locks you in until the police show up.

In the film, Sarah and Meg are spending their first night in the new house when, as bad luck would have it, three men break in. They are searching for the millions of dollars that were supposedly hidden in the house by its former owner, a reclusive billionaire. There are many tense and scary moments during this game-of-cat-and-mouse film, but, of course, Meg and Sarah are safe in the end.

The film debuted at number one at the box office on its opening weekend, earning more than $30 million. It went on to earn nearly $100 million worldwide. Kristen definitely caught the attention of the critics, many of whom pointed out the uncanny resemblance between Jodie and Kristen. The two of them really could be mother and daughter!

Kristen and Jodie turned out to be perfect for

their roles, but neither of them were actually cast in the movie at first! The role of Meg originally went to Oscar-winning actress Nicole Kidman, who had to drop out due to an injury, while pretty blond actress Hayden Panettiere, best known for her role as high school cheerleader Claire Bennet on the NBC science-fiction drama *Heroes*, was originally cast as Sarah, but was eventually replaced by Kristen, who more closely resembled Jodie.

Kristen had a great time on the set, and learned a ton from her talented costars. Even though Jodie Foster is a well-respected movie star known all over the world, Kristen doesn't recall being intimidated by her. "I was an overly confident 10-year-old, I guess. I was aware enough to note how important the people I was working with [on *Panic Room*] were, but I was also kind of aware that I was just a kid and people don't expect anything from kids—you know, just know your lines and stay in focus. So if I did anything remotely good, people would be really surprised and appreciative. That was kind of cool," she explained to the *Star-Ledger*.

Though there's no denying Kristen learned

a ton from her talented costar. The pair got along well, and Jodie was a great example for Kristen. "We got along so well, though. It helped a lot to just sit and watch [Jodie], because she's so amazing. She's completely professional and she knows everyone's name on the crew and she's always on time. She was great," Kristen told *Time for Kids*. Kristen even identified Jodie as someone in show business who she really looked up to. "[Because] she's not just an actress. [She's] a director, she's a producer, she's a writer. She's conquered the business. You don't see her much in the press. She's very, very well respected, very professional. She's awesome."

Perhaps Jodie Foster had a much deeper impact on Kristen than the ten-year-old realized at the time. Several years and several movies later, she described Jodie in a way that very much mirrored the path Kristen's own acting career had taken. "[Jodie] does what she believes. She doesn't do anything that she doesn't want to do. She does the stories she wants to do. She's not going to compromise, and you do well when you do things you want to do," Kristen said to hollywood.com.

Panic Room was a pivotal moment in Kristen's career—the success of the movie meant she was starting to become a household name, and she had found someone in Hollywood to look up to. Plus, Kristen got something else really special from that movie that she didn't have before—an award nomination!

Kristen was nominated for a Young Artist Award for her work on *Panic Room*—her very first award nomination! It was for the category of Best Performance in a Feature Film—Leading Young Actress. The Young Artist Awards recognize young artists under the age of eighteen in television, movies, theater, and music. Although she didn't win—Alexa Vega from *Spy Kids 2: Island of Lost Dreams* did— Kristen was nominated in the company of some noted up-and-coming actresses, including Nickelodeon star Amanda Bynes, *Across the Universe* actress Evan Rachel Wood, and America Ferrera, best known for playing the role of Betty Suarez on the hit TV show *Ugly Betty*. Once Kristen had a taste of what it was like to be recognized for her work, she couldn't get enough, and she quickly moved on to her next project.

In 2003, Kristen was cast in another psychological thriller, *Cold Creek Manor*, in the role of Kristen Tilson, a young daughter in a family that decides to give up city life and move to the country. Kristen's parents buy a crumbling old mansion and, unbeknownst to them, hire the former owner, who has just been released from prison, to help with the renovations. He begins terrorizing the family, who work to uncover his dark secret and save themselves from his sinister plan to take back his house.

Unlike *Panic Room, Cold Creek Manor* was not a box office success, despite the fact that two well-known actors—Dennis Quaid and Sharon Stone—were cast in the film's leading roles. But working on the movie did add another notch on Kristen's constantly-growing acting résumé! Plus, it garnered her a second Youth Artist Award nomination—this time, in the category of Best Performance in a Feature Film—Supporting Young Actress. Unfortunately, she didn't win the award this time, either, but the fact that she was nominated, despite the movie's unsuccessful run at the box office, proved that Kristen truly had star power. And lucky for her, another huge opportunity was just around the corner!

CHAPTER 3
Slowly Becoming a Star

Kristen had already mastered acting in supporting roles in movies—now she wanted a shot at being the star! And she did just that in 2004 when she landed her first starring role in the children's action-comedy *Catch That Kid*, opposite two other young stars: Max Thieriot, who has appeared in family-friendly films like *The Pacifier*, *Nancy Drew*, and *Kit Kittredge: An American Girl*, and Corbin Bleu, best known for his headlining role as the singing and dancing basketball cocaptain Chad Danforth in Disney's *High School Musical* series. At the time, however, Corbin was a lot like Kristen—just another young actor hoping to make it big!

In *Catch That Kid*, Stewart's character, Maddy Phillips, is an athletic twelve-year-old who excels at mountain climbing like her father had—that is, before he fell on his way down from climbing Mount

Everest. His injuries ultimately—but unexpectedly—paralyze him. An experimental procedure offered in Denmark might help him, but the family will never know because the operation costs a quarter of a million dollars, which the family doesn't have.

With the help of her two best friends, Austin, a computer geek, and Gus, a go-kart mechanic, Maddy masterminds a bank heist to pay for the surgery. Of course, each of the kids' respective talents helps them along the way!

The *Chicago Sun-Times* applauded the movie, calling it "well-made, straightforward and entertaining." They also called Kristen out for her excellent performance, calling it "stalwart and sure" and predicting that her "plucky heroine will win the hearts of . . . young audiences." And win hearts she did!

The *San Francisco Chronicle* also lavished high praise on Kristen's girl hero character: "As Maddy, Kristen Stewart is a kick-butt, take-no-stuff winner who makes it all happen . . . [She] is perfect as Maddy. She has that Avril Lavigne 'girl power' look down. She is buffed enough to look like she really could climb sheer walls, and she even walks like a jock. There are others on the screen, but this is Stewart's movie." It was high praise for Kristen, and she definitely earned it.

While not a box office smash, *Catch That Kid* allowed Kristen to show yet another side of her versatile acting skills and also exposed her to family audiences. And she really enjoyed the opportunity to perform her own stunts, such as climbing up a water tower. Not to mention the fact that she loved the experience of getting to be the star of a film, instead of a supporting character.

On the heels of that family-friendly film came a very different role—the kind that shows Kristen's ability, perhaps even her need, to "mix it up" as far as choosing film projects.

This part was in a 2004 cable television film called *Speak*, and Kristen had a starring role. Based on the award-winning novel of the same name by popular young adult author Laurie Halse Anderson, *Speak* is the story of a thirteen-year-old high school freshman named Melinda Sordino who is physically assaulted by a male upperclassman and, as a result of this horribly traumatizing experience, pretty much stops communicating with others, including her parents. Although Melinda doesn't speak many lines to others in the movie, she keeps up a sarcastic, dark-witted running commentary in her head throughout the film. And eventually, she finds emotional refuge in the art class taught by a free-spirited teacher named Mr. Freeman and physical refuge in an unused storage closet, where she reflects on the night of the assault and tries to deal with the emotions.

As the school year progresses, and with some help from her lab partner Dave—played by Michael Angarano, who went on to become Kristen's boyfriend (they met while making this movie!), Melinda slowly begins to regain her self-confidence. And at the end, she is able to confront the boy who hurt her. And although it's clear that she still needs time to recover, the fact that she found the courage to finally speak up is empowering, and sparks the healing process.

The movie was a critical success. The *Hollywood Reporter* called it a "well-made and extremely touching drama." And once again, praise was heaped on Kristen for her expert and authentic handling of the character. "Much of the credit goes to Kristen Stewart, who plays the girl in an understated performance that will touch everyone who sees it," the *Hollywood Reporter* raved. Kristen felt privileged to bring the main character from this popular novel to life, and truly put everything she had into the character. And it paid off!

The year 2004 was a busy one for the young star. As soon as filming for *Speak* wrapped, Kristen threw herself into her next role, the psychological thriller *Undertow*. Kristen portrayed Lila, the girlfriend of young leading actor Jamie Bell, who played one of two young boys on the run from a murderous uncle.

Kristen's performance in this film led to a third Youth Artist Award nomination—once again in the category of Best Performance in a Feature Film—Supporting Young Actress. For the third straight year, she failed to win—but clearly Hollywood was taking notice of her.

Kristen's next project—the 2005 fantasy space adventure film *Zathura: A Space Adventure*—put her back in front of family audiences. The movie was based on a children's book written by award-winning author Chris Van Allsburg, who also penned the classic stories *The Polar Express* and *Jumanji*.

Kristen played the part of Lisa, the crabby and negligent older sister of two little boys, Walter and Danny, who discover a board game called Zathura hidden in their house. The game plunges its players—and the house—into the depths of outer space where they encounter meteors, reptile-like creatures called Zorgons, a nomadic astronaut, a robot, and lots of other surprises.

Director Jon Favreau was very complimentary about his young female lead. "We auditioned a lot of people [Kristen's] age for *Zathura*, and . . . [she] really stood out as having a presence, and a look, and chops, and poise. Most young girls or boys have sort of an unfocused, scattered energy. [She has] a very still energy to [her]," he raved to *Interview* magazine.

While the movie was praised by critics, Kristen's particular performance didn't earn her as much attention as her previous films because her character was actually in a state of suspended animation for much of the movie. (Early on in the film, the wrong move on the game's board renders her frozen into an icy statue!)

Kristen's role as a frozen girl required her to have a full body cast made of herself—a totally surreal experience which, according to her, is something you couldn't understand unless you have an identical twin! Kristen told teenhollywood.com that making the cast was a painstaking process: "It was a three step process. The first was a digital scan of my body that they entered into a computer . . . [Then] they molded, individually, each part of my body . . . The last step in the process was painting her. I went in and stood next to my mannequin basically and they painted every nuance of my face. Every freckle on my arm is on that body. There's no difference." Talk about a crazy—and unique—experience!

Zathura had a fairly big budget and wide release, but Kristen's next project was a lot different. She returned once again to her indie roots with another film released in 2005—*Fierce People*—in which she played Maya, the granddaughter of a billionaire, played by Donald Sutherland. Maya is the love interest of the young male lead character Finn.

It was Kristen's first romantic role, which was, of course, a very valuable experience for the up-and-coming star. And even though Kristen had to portray someone in love, she never felt out of her comfort zone. "[Maya and Finn's] relationship is really innocent, very fresh and sweet. None of it was ever weird or awkward," Kristen told *Interview* magazine.

In the movie, sixteen-year-old Finn just wants to spend the summer in South America, where the anthropologist father he's never met is studying the Iskanani Indians, or 'Fierce People,' a primitive tribe who live in the jungles of the Amazon rain forest. Instead, Finn gets arrested trying to help his mother, and the two of them eventually move into a house on the estate of a billionaire to try to get their lives on track. However, as mother and son soon come to realize, the lives of the super-rich are every bit as "fierce" and mysterious as that of a tribe of native jungle dwellers! The film was a lot of fun for Kristen, and further cemented her status as an "indie" queen.

With *Zathura* and *Fierce People*, Kristen proved she could go from big-screen star to indie princess in a blink of an eye. Her star was rising fast!

CHAPTER 4
Breakout Year

Ultimately, 2004, 2005, and 2006 were big years for the young star, but they were nothing compared to 2007! Kristen put her career into overdrive that year and appeared in five films!

First up was a leading role in the romantic drama *In the Land of Women*. Her character, Lucy Hardwicke, was the love interest of the male lead, Carter Webb. Carter was played by Adam Brody, who is best known for playing the charming and cute Seth Cohen on the FOX teen drama *The O.C.*

Meg Ryan starred as Lucy's mother, Sarah Hardwicke, and Olympia Dukakis was Carter's eccentric grandmother.

In the story, Carter is a would-be screenwriter trying to live a Hollywood life when he is dumped by his movie star girlfriend. At a crossroads, he decides to spend a few weeks back in the Midwest with his possibly dying—and hilariously cranky—grandmother to help her out while recovering from his romantic heartbreak.

The Hardwickes are the family across the street, each of whom has her own problems. The movie follows the relationships that Carter develops with each of the three very different women.

The movie got mixed reviews, but what *wasn't* mixed were the reviews of Kristen's performance! *Variety* offered glowing praise of the young star and wrote ". . . [Kristen's] coltish vulnerability as Lucy Hardwicke was the movie's high point." This meant a lot coming from such a long-running and well-respected magazine, and it was a good way for Kristen to start off 2007.

Kristen is a big fan of horror movies—her all-time favorite is *The Shining,* starring Jack Nicholson—so it was no surprise when she picked a supernatural thriller as her next project. The film was called *The Messengers,* and Kristen played the lead character, Jess Solomon, a troubled teenager who moves with her family to a peaceful sunflower farm in rural North Dakota. But the bright, beautiful outside looks so different compared to the dark, scary things that happen inside the house.

Jess and her little brother Ben, who is mute, not only see ghosts—they are attacked by them! And their parents aren't any help because they don't believe Jess, and little Ben can't speak.

Kristen admits that even though she loves horror movies, she's actually afraid of ghosts. "Ever since I've been a kid, I've been absolutely, totally scared of ghosts. Like whenever I would run around my house terrified when I was five years old, it was always because of ghosts," she told moviesonline.ca.

But it's the wait-for-it part of horror flicks that Kristen enjoys most, and possibly the reason why she wanted to work on this film in the first place: "I like when all of a sudden you're watching a movie and it slows down and you're like, 'Oh my god, something's definitely going to happen' and you know it, but even when it does, it still scares you just as much," she explained to moviesonline.ca.

Kristen continued on to say that she actually had a "trippy experience" in her hotel room during the filming of *The Messengers*: "I opened my eyes and this image of this woman just filled my entire view . . . [I] let out the most gut wrenching scream. I mean people called the hotel room to see if I was okay."

Of course she was just fine—but how scary is that?! Perhaps when you're an actor, it's sometimes hard to leave your character behind when you finish filming for the day.

Another film Kristen made in 2007 was called *The Cake Eaters*, an independent feature that was also the directorial debut of television and film actress Mary Stuart Masterson.

The movie is a small-town drama with an ensemble cast of characters representing two families the Kimbroughs and Kaminskis—whose lives are interconnected by love and loss. Kristen played Georgia Kaminski, a teenager with a debilitating terminal disease called Friedriech's Ataxia, who is determined to fall in love with a boy before she dies.

Kristen described the project to about.com as ". . . a really quaint little movie [that] is . . . madly triumphant [and has an] unabashedly outward sense of hope."

Mary Stuart Masterson, who also started doing movies at a young age, had Kristen in mind for the role of Georgia from the beginning. She gushed to moviesonline.ca: "[I] was instantly struck with [Kristen's] tremendous intelligence and also her sense of herself. She was truly grounded and has a power and ferocity about her that is so perfect for [the character of Georgia] and yet in this delicate body that was also necessary to play the role. I met her and I just knew."

One point that the film drove home for Kristen was the need to live life to the fullest, regardless of what might get in the way. "That was the theme on my particular aspect of the story," she explained to MTV.com. "If you're going to live however long you're going to live, you have to live and not focus on the negative aspects. And [those suffering from terminal illnesses] are so good at that, they have a remarkable appreciation for their lives. It is something to be envied." It was a great lesson for the young actress to learn, and possibly one of the reasons why she took the project on in the first place. And as usual, Kristen charmed the critics.

The renowned movie critic Roger Ebert even called Kristen's performance "remarkable" in the *Chicago Sun-Times*!

Next, Kristen played a supporting role in bubbly blond actress Kate Hudson's writing and directorial debut, *Cutlass*. The sixteen-minute short film is a trip down memory lane for the main character Robin, who was played by actress Virginia Madsen. Robin is an adult, but there are lots of scenes of her looking back on her childhood. A bleached blond Kristen played the young Robin in the flashbacks, and one of her future *Twilight* costars, Dakota Fanning (who plays the pixie-like but powerful Volturi vampire Jane in the second installment of the series) stars as adult Robin's daughter Lacy. Even though it was a short film, Kristen enjoyed working with talented actresses like Kate, Virginia, and Dakota. But she didn't have time to reflect on her experiences for long. Kristen, being who she is, was onto the next project!

And her next project was something she was really excited about. She was slated to play another starring role in an independent movie, this one called *Adventureland.* Written and directed by Greg Mottola of *Superbad* fame, the semi-autobiographical coming-of-age comedy takes place in 1987 in a ramshackle old mom-and-pop amusement park, just like the one Greg worked at as a teenager! The movie filmed on location in Pennsylvania at an amusement park called Kennywood, which you can visit if you're ever in the Pittsburgh area!

Kristen played the role of Em Lewin, a long-time employee of the park who Kristen called "terribly introverted and damaged" to about.com. "I could imagine what it would be like to not like yourself very much and not have a mom and not have a dad to reassure you, and sort of be kicking it alone and feel like you're sort of smarter than everyone but no one gets it. I get all of that," she continued to about.com. Playing this role was probably difficult for Kristen, who comes from a tight-knit family, but it was probably also what attracted her to the role the most!

Whether or not Kristen thought she could play the role, writer and director Greg Mottola knew she was perfect for it from the very beginning. He told

USA Today that the character of Em "needed to be complicated and needed to be truly conflicted. We needed an actress who [could] convey a really believable sense of strength. I knew with Kristen that character wouldn't just be a brat. With Kristen, you can't dismiss her that easily. She's no pushover." Greg actually cast Kristen without even having her audition! His reason was simple: "She's got a quality. I personally find her very fascinating to watch. She's someone who makes thinking dramatic," Greg told moviesonline.ca.

Adventureland was actually filming when Kristen got the call about doing an audition for *Twilight*. Greg laughingly recalled to blackbookmag. com a conversation he had with Kristen about the audition: "And Kristen is so mellow, she was just like, 'Yeah, it's a vampire movie. It's cool.' And then one day she's like, 'Yeah, I got that part. You know, could be pretty cool' . . . Like, not a big deal about it at all."

Luckily, it ended up being a *very* big deal—because having Kristen's name attached to *Twilight* helped *Adventureland* get some major press it might not have gotten otherwise. Although the movie was filmed in 2007, it didn't get released until early 2009, right in between the release of *Twilight* in theaters and on DVD.

Adventureland earned a great deal of critical acclaim, especially for Kristen. The *Los Angeles Times* noted that "Stewart, who has a gift for investing completely in her characters, brings so much intensity to her part that she turns this [film] on its head by making Em's problems the film's most compelling."

And Roger Ebert of the *Chicago Sun-Times* admiringly called Kristen "an actress ready to do important things."

Kristen really enjoyed shooting *Adventureland*— who wouldn't love filming in an amusement park? But the experience also helped Kristen overcome a childhood fear of amusement parks. "I was always afraid of Disneyland," she laughingly told MTV.com. "Because there was an urban legend that they used to steal the kids and shave their heads. They'd take them out of the parks, and then the park would shut down [in an emergency] to try to find the bald child. I never wanted to be that child!"

Greg Mottola's inspiration for *Adventureland* came from his own life experiences, and the movie also has an underlying theme about thinking about what you want to do in life and being prepared if the course you've charted for yourself suddenly throws you off-course. This might make *Twilight* fans wonder—what would Kristen have done if she hadn't become an actress?

The answer is—she's not sure!

"I don't know what I'd do. I'd have a lot of pent-up energy I'd have to throw at something and, if it wasn't this, it would be very unsatisfying because . . . I'm not very good at anything else. I'm bad with my hands. I can't make things. My head is far from organized, so I wouldn't be good at a desk job," she told film.com.

While Kristen's fans would probably disagree that she wouldn't be good at other things, they are probably thrilled to know she isn't going to take time off from acting anytime soon!

Kristen's final project in 2007 was her biggest—and, ultimately, most important. She ended the year with a bang by playing a supporting role in the critically acclaimed, Oscar-nominated film *Into the Wild*, starring the hot, young actor Emile Hirsch of *Lords of Dogtown* and *Speed Racer* fame.

Based on the book of the same name by Jon Krakauer, a writer and legendary mountain climber, *Into the Wild* tells the story of an affluent honors student named Christopher McCandless who, upon his graduation from college, chooses to give away all of his money and possessions to go live in the Alaskan wilderness.

In the film, Kristen plays Tracy Tatro, a free-spirited singer who lives in a bohemian community in the California desert known as Slab City. She falls for the handsome and idealistic young adventurer, played by Emile.

Both for her audition and in the film, Kristen played guitar and sang. For her audition for director Sean Penn, she played the Beatles song "Blackbird." "I botched it," she told *People* magazine. "But he called me later and said, 'Do you want to do this [role]?' And I was like—yeah!" In the actual film, Kristen had to play in front of a live audience—something she'd never done before! The audience was made up of the actual residents of Slab City. "I've never played music for anyone," she confessed to moviesonline.ca. "But they were a very warm crowd—they were clapping and stoked to be there. That made it a lot of fun."

Kristen loved getting the opportunity to play guitar on the set of *Into the Wild*. But if you're wondering if she has plans to release an album in the future, the answer is—no! Kristen told *CosmoGirl*, "If there was ever a film that was musically inclined, I would absolutely be there and down! I love music and I've always played guitar. But no, I'm definitely not cutting a record. There are really cool people I've been playing with lately, but there won't be a Kristen Stewart album!"

Playing music wasn't the only great thing about Kristen's role in *Into the Wild*. The film was a hit at the box office and with the critics. *Rolling Stone* called *Into the Wild* a "beautiful, wrenching film," and the *Chicago Tribune*'s review of the movie singled out Kristen as having done "vividly well with a sketch of a role."

And the *New York Times* had some serious praise

for her: "As the child-woman whose longing for the ill-fated wanderer Christopher McCandless is largely expressed through piercing looks and sensitive strumming, Ms. Stewart gave form and feeling to the possibility that the search for freedom and authentic experiences can be found in the embrace of another human being. This was a girl worth living for, if not for that film's lost soul."

Her turn as hippie-chick Tracy was the latest in an impressive lineup of playing troubled adolescent characters. Kristen stands out in the industry as a real teenager who can skillfully and genuinely portray a—well, *real* teenager—complete with typical teen traits: moodiness, recklessness, and awkwardness.

When it comes to choosing her movie roles, Kristen says she is drawn to stories that she can personally connect with. She told the *Star-Ledger* that there are a lot of "cheesy scripts" out there about adolescence: "There's a lot of material floating around that's sort of empty. And I can't really work on something like that. I can only be a part of something that feels like, if I don't bring this character to life she's going to die right there on the page."

It's not a parent or an agent or a manager that guides Kristen in her decisions. She trusts her gut. "I commit to projects that do something to my stomach. It's all about what it does to your stomach when you read it," she told blackbookmag.com.

Mary Stuart Masterson, Kristen's director in *The Cake Eaters*, has a lot of respect for the young star and predicts that she will have a brilliant future. "I think she's strong and lovely and [very] smart . . . and will choose her roles carefully and will do fantastically well for many, many, many years," she told moviesonline.ca.

When it comes to acting, it's something Kristen feels she has to do. "Acting is such a personal thing, which is weird because at the same time, it's not. It's for the consumption of other people. But in terms of creative outlets and expressing yourself, it's just the most extreme version of that that I've ever found . . . [and] when you get to study something else and understand someone else and completely lose yourself in it, you feel a certain responsibility. Or at least I do, because if you don't bring that character to life the right way, then nobody else gets to see them or experience what you did," she told the *Los Angeles Times* blog.

Kristen finds the creative process of acting very satisfying. "There's something really instantaneous the second you do a scene and you feel it and it's so real for you and you know it's down and you nailed it," she explained to moviesonline.ca. "It's so amazing just because you've told the story and you did it . . . [When] you nail it, it just feels so good."

With five movies completed in 2007, it had certainly been Kristen's most prolific year. She was only seventeen years old at the time. But Kristen was not one to rest on what she had already accomplished. She was always looking ahead to the next big thing, which in this case, happened to be 2008! Turns out, 2008 was just as big—if not bigger—than 2007.

First on Kristen's plate was a cameo appearance in the science-fiction action movie *Jumper*. The movie follows the plight of a young man named David Rice—played by the supercute Hayden Christiensen, the young Anakin Skywalker in the Star Wars saga—who discovers he is capable of teleporting himself, or "jumping," to any location. He also discovers that a secret society is out to kill him. Kristen played a supporting character, Sophie, who is David's younger half sister.

Jumper was a reunion of sorts for Kristen, as the cast included several actors with whom she'd previously worked: Max Thieriot from *Catch That Kid*; Jamie Bell from *Undertow*; and Diane Lane from *Fierce People*.

After that, Kristen was cast in another supporting role. She played Zoe, the rebellious daughter of Robert DeNiro's character Ben, a stressed-out movie producer, in an independent movie called *What Just Happened*. Kristen's director from *Into the Wild*, Sean Penn, starred in the movie, too—as himself!

And finally, Kristen completed yet another indie film—*The Yellow Handkerchief*—in which she plays a lost and lonely teenage girl named Martine who embarks on a road trip to New Orleans with two other misfits—a geeky young man and a middle-aged ex-convict.

But it was Kristen's portrayal of Isabella "Bella" Swan—in what she thought was going to be a "little cult vampire movie"—that would come to define her year, and quite possibly her career.

CHAPTER 5
Little Miss Sunshine State

Ashley Michele Greene was born on February 21, 1987, in Jacksonville, Florida.

The largest city in the Sunshine State, Jacksonville was originally named Cowford, before being renamed in 1822 after future president Andrew Jackson. Jackson had served as the first military governor of the Florida territory after the United States acquired it from Spain.

Ashley's parents were very proud when their first daughter was born. Her father, Joe, was the owner of a concrete construction business. Ashley's mom, Michele, worked for an insurance company. But the person who was probably most excited about Ashley's birth was her brother, Joe, who's only a year and a half older than Ashley. He must have been pretty happy to finally have somebody to play with! And now that the two of them are older, they're super close. So close, in fact, that Joe bought his very own *Twilight* T-shirt to wear to support his little sis. He was even Ashley's date to the Hollywood premiere of *Twilight*—which was an incredible experience, even though photographers were yelling at the poor guy to get out of the picture! Now, Ashley is hoping that Joe will move to L.A. and try his hand at acting. Ashley told about.com: " . . . my brother's one of my very good friends . . . We have a lot to talk about *now*. Before I think when I was a teenager it was really, 'Whatever.' But yeah, I talk to my brother. He's actually interested in acting a little bit and so it's really cool to see his little sister go through what I'm going through."

But before she was a big star walking the red carpet with her older brother, Ashley was just a regular kid. Ashley attended University Christian School, a private school in Jacksonville, before transferring to Samuel W. Wolfson High School, also in Jacksonville, in the tenth grade. Growing up, Ashley was a self-described "good kid" who kept busy with cheerleading, both for University Christian and for an all-star squad that competed outside of school. But Ashley wasn't *just* a cheerleader: She also kicked butt at tae kwon do and took acting and dance classes. Though at this point, her acting classes were mostly for fun. To earn some pocket money, Ashley worked as a hostess at a restaurant in Jacksonville named Copeland's and—no surprise here!—did some modeling. On top of all that, she was also an honors student. Her parents must have been pretty pleased with their bright and beautiful daughter—and rightfully so!

One of Ashley's favorite high school memories was going to the senior prom—not her own, but her then-boyfriend's. She remembers the night well because she wore an incredible dress that she paid for with her own pocket money! "I wore this amazing gold dress but it was a little risqué so my mom was like, 'You have to wear something like a scarf or else your dad isn't going to let you out of the house.' My dad would've been like 'no way' because the neckline plunged. But it was tight, so nothing was falling out. The whole thing was just gold sequins all the way down but it was like a shade between a lighter gold and bronze. I fell in love with it. I bought it myself because my mom [wouldn't]. I did my hair in a kind of . . . almost like a goddess hair style with a bunch of little ringlets and headband to match it. It was really pretty. I had so much fun," she reminisced to *Teen* magazine. Looks like Ashley was channeling Alice's love of fashion at an early age!

Ashley admits that she "fell" into acting, and that, growing up, she didn't have any concrete dreams of being a famous actress. This probably contributed to Ashley's really "normal" childhood. In an interview with Ashley's hometown newspaper, the *Florida Times-Union*, her older brother, Joe, said his sister hadn't been one of those kids who was always performing at home in front of the family's video camera. In fact, she wasn't even really involved in theater in middle school or high school. Instead, Ashley wanted to be a model. She could have easily done it—she was a stunning girl with dark hair and dark brown eyes, and a unique look that people everywhere were always complimenting her on. But at only five feet five inches, she was told she wasn't tall enough for runway modeling, which has a minimum height requirement of five feet seven inches. So instead of focusing all of her energy on making it as a model, Ashley took an acting class that specialized in commercial work in hopes of getting work in television commercials.

Though she started out on a lark, it didn't take long for Ashley to get bitten by the acting bug! "[The] teacher who I was taught by was just so passionate about it. He was amazing!" Ashley told *MediaBlvd* magazine. "I fell in love with [acting], instantly. I was like, 'This is so what I want to do! I don't want to model.'"

Typical Ashley, she put everything she had into perfecting her acting. And soon enough, she started talking about moving out west to California. She did some research and found an agent and a manager, which was a huge step in the right direction. But unfortunately, they told her she needed to relocate to Hollywood if she ever wanted to get any jobs. There just weren't a lot of opportunities for aspiring actors in Florida. So at the young age of seventeen, Ashley made the very grown-up decision to graduate from high school early and move to California to pursue her dream of acting.

Luckily, being the great student that she was, Ashley had enough credits to graduate, so she left high school a semester early with a diploma in hand and headed to Hollywood. Fortunately, Ashley had a few friends from Jacksonville who were also aspiring actresses, and they agreed to make the move with her, in hopes of jump-starting their own careers.

But what about Ashley's family? Even though she was only seventeen, Ashley's parents supported her decision. "I was really passionate about [acting]," Ashley said to *MediaBlvd* magazine. "I guess my parents saw that, and they were really supportive." Even though they let her go, her parents were, of course, worried. Ashley was a smart and responsible young woman who had a good head on her shoulders, but she was still very young to be out on her own, thousands of miles away from home. "It was scary," her mom, Michele, told the *Florida Times-Union*. "There were a lot of late nights where we lay in bed and talked about it. But it's kind of a Catch-22: If you raise your kid to follow their dreams, you're kind of on the hook."

Ashley knew she was taking a big step in moving

so far away to chase a dream that she might never catch, but she recognized that her parents were taking a huge step, too. "I think it was more gutsy for my parents than it was for me," she recalled to the *Florida Times-Union.* "It was what I wanted to do; it seemed logical to me. But my parents, for them to think, 'Oh yeah, we'll support you doing that at seventeen'—that was a gutsy move for them. A lot of parents thought they were crazy, but they trusted me."

And it was a good thing Ashley's parents got on board with her dream, because her family's love and support has always been very important to her. "I am really close to my family—my mom, my dad and my brother," she told *MediaBlvd* magazine. "My mom and dad are still together, and I had a very solid foundation and upbringing. They're really supportive, and I love them to death." At the end of the day, Ashley's parents probably knew their little girl would be fine out there, because she had a strong foundation of support from her family. Plus, if things ever got too tough, Ashley knew she always had the best backup plan she could ever ask for:

moving back home with her loving family. But it turns out, she never needed her backup plan—plan A worked just fine!

CHAPTER 6

Getting Settled, Getting Started

After Ashley's bags were packed and all the arrangements were made, Ashley's mother accompanied her on the trip out to California to help her get settled into an apartment. She helped with things like arranging for hot water and electricity in the apartment—things that Ashley had no idea how to do! She realized that she—and probably most kids her age—didn't have a clue how easy life was when you lived with your parents. But even after she returned to Florida, Michele continued to help her daughter by giving her directions around Los Angeles over the phone when Ashley got lost going to auditions or other appointments. Talk about a great mom!

Michele could help her daughter with lots of things, but unfortunately, she couldn't help her book acting jobs. In the beginning, Ashley struggled, and success was slow in coming. In fact, Ashley says that she had such bad luck at first that several times her father almost made her come home!

And, of course, living away from home at such a young age also provided its fair share of temptations, forcing Ashley to make some tough choices as far as her future. "You're 17. There are no adults. It's L.A. And so I went through this stage where I would just go out, not be responsible, not focus on work or class, and my management was like, 'Listen, you could go either way. You could be this person—I won't name names, [but she's] a reality show actress. Or you could go this way—[she's an] award-winning actress.' That was a real shock," Ashley told *Nylon* magazine.

This was the wake-up call Ashley needed to straighten up and continue chasing her dream of making it as an actress. Even though Ashley was probably discouraged sometimes, she persevered, because she comes across as someone who tries to see the bright side of every situation. You can tell this about Ashley just by looking at her 2005 senior picture from the Wolfson High School yearbook.

It contains lyrics from singer Avril Lavigne's song "Who Knows": *Who knows what can happen—do what ya do, just keep on laughing—Find yourself— there's always a brand new day.* Talk about a great attitude—an important thing to have when you're trying to break into the difficult world of show business!

Ashley's brother had faith that his baby sister would hit it big eventually. "I think we all had confidence that she had all the skills and attitude to be one of the people who actually makes it out there, that it's something she'd fall into. She's always been a social butterfly. Even though she's pretty, she's still real nice," Joe told the *Florida Times-Union.*

Ashley stuck it out, and eventually, she did land something! For her first two years in L.A., she spent a lot of time getting adjusted to living on her own and doing guest roles on movies and TV shows. She also continued to work as a model and did work for fengjunk.com, an online boutique known for its ecletic and trendsetting fashion accessories; Stop Staring!, a California boutique that specializes in vintage cocktail dresses inspired by glamorous silver screen icons such as Audrey Hepburn (one of Ashley's faves!); and Wendy Glez, a designer of fabulously feminine lingerie and loungewear.

For her first acting gig, Ashley actually played a role on *Punk'd*, the hit MTV reality show created by hottie actor and master prankster, Ashton Kutcher, that pulls off elaborate pranks on unsuspecting big-name celebs!

In Ashley's episode, she played the role of an underage clubber who's partied a little too hard and, as a result, gets supercute actor Justin Long into hot water with the law! Now that's an awesome first role! "It was fun," Ashley reported to *Teen Vogue*. "[Justin] freaked out."

That was Ashley's first television role, but not her last. She also made guest appearances on the television dramas *Crossing Jordan* and *Shark*. Starring Jill Hennessy, *Crossing Jordan* follows a team of medical examiners as they work with the Boston Police Department to solve murders. Ashley appeared on the show in its fifth season—2006—in an episode titled "The Elephant in the Room" as a young murder victim named Ann Rappaport.

Shark is a legal drama starring James Woods as a former high profile defense attorney turned cutthroat prosecutor for the Los Angeles district attorney's crime unit. Ashley had a very small part as a background character named Natalie Faber in a 2008 episode called "Partners in Crime." And she had a small recurring role in a short-lived primetime soap series called *Desire*. The show, which aired from September to December 2006, was about two brothers named Alex and Louis Thomas who are on the run from a mobster family in New Jersey and relocate to Los Angeles, where they find work at a restaurant. Ashley played a supporting character named Renata in seven episodes.

In between television projects, Ashley won a small role in the 2007 independent film *King of California* starring Michael Douglas and Nikki Reed's *Thirteen* costar, Evan Rachel Wood. In the movie, Evan Rachel Wood's character, Miranda, is a sixteen-year-old working at McDonald's to support herself after being abandoned by her mother and while her father is away in a mental institution. Adorable Ashley plays a mildly obnoxious McDonald's customer who places a very detailed order with Miranda, including a request for a "McFlurry with extra Oreos, and make sure they stir it in."

Ashley also appeared in a 2008 horror-comedy called *Otis* about a sloppy, overweight, forty-year-old pizza delivery man named Otis who kidnaps pretty teenage girls in hopes of creating the perfect prom date that he never actually had. He calls all his kidnapped victims Kim. Ashley played Kim Number Four!

Working as a guest star was a great experience for the relatively unknown actress, but Ashley was still on the lookout for her big break, the role that would cement her as a household name in Hollywood. Little did she know that the very next project she'd audition for would catapult her career into the stratosphere!

CHAPTER 7
Growing Up Fast

Cheryl Houston and her husband Seth Reed were thrilled when their beautiful baby girl Nicole "Nikki" Houston Reed was born on May 17, 1988, in their hometown of Los Angeles, California.

Cheryl was a beautician, and Seth was a set designer who has worked on a lot of well-known films. Some of those films include *Valkyrie* and *Minority Report*, both starring Tom Cruise, *Blades of Glory* with Will Ferrell and Jon Heder (of *Napoleon Dynamite* fame), and *Lords of Dogtown*, one of the first movies Nikki would eventually be cast in!

But before she was a star, Nikki was just a regular California girl. And unfortunately, being a regular kid has its share of ups and downs. One of the downs that Nikki had to deal with at a very young age was her parents' divorce. Cheryl and Seth divorced when Nikki was just two years old, so she spent her childhood living with her mother and older brother, Nathan, who is two years older than Nikki and currently attends UCLA. (She also has a younger half brother with autism.)

Nikki and Cheryl's relationship was not an easy one. Nikki has said that her mother did not establish many rules to follow and that she and Nathan were given a good deal of freedom at a very young age. "My mother didn't know how to raise kids and was just as confused as us," Nikki told usatoday.com in an online chat. Even though she didn't establish a ton of rules, Cheryl still loved her daughter and worked hard to provide for her. "My mom and dad both worked so hard. We never got help with homework and didn't have family meals, but there was a lot of love in the house," Nikki continued in her interview with usatoday.com.

Nikki was only five years old when her father started dating a woman who would become a very important influence in Nikki's life. That woman's name was Catherine Hardwicke—the future director of *Twilight* and the director and cowriter of the very first movie Nikki worked on, *Thirteen*. Even though Catherine and Seth eventually broke up, she remained close to Nikki and was very influential in helping Nikki get into acting. Nikki not only starred in Catherine's movie *Thirteen*, about the life of a modern teenage girl, but the movie was also loosely based on Nikki's own life as a teenager.

When Nikki entered her early teenage years, she transformed into what some might call a "wild child." She started hanging out with a fast crowd, and her priorities changed. Things like hair and makeup became more important to her than hitting the books. She made bad choices when it came to boys, clothes, and her behavior. She went from a cute, pigtailed pixie to someone who seemed angry a lot, and who only seemed to care about looking pretty and having a good time with her friends. "When I was with [my friends], I thought I had everything," she told the *New York Daily News*. "I would walk down the hall [at school] like I was queen of the world. It was an invincible feeling. I thought I knew who I was." But when those "friends" got kicked out of school for their bad behavior, all of a sudden Nikki felt very alone.

Catherine noticed the differences in Nikki right away. She told the *New York Daily News*, "Even as a 5-year-old, Nikki was so open and funny, totally willing to take risks. When she started changing from 12 to 13 years old, I saw her losing her joy. She became so angry. It really freaked me out. I wanted her to get back to creative, rather than destructive, things."

Catherine cared a lot about Nikki, so she tried to think of ways to help Nikki navigate this very tough time in her life. She knew Nikki would listen to her, because even though she and Seth were no longer together, Nikki and Catherine were still close.

And as far as Nikki was concerned, Catherine was the one person she trusted completely.

"I always knew I could go to her when I needed someone," Nikki told the British newspaper the *Independent*. "I guess I just hit rock bottom and had absolutely nobody. Once again, Catherine was there to help me through it."

So when Nikki happened to mention an interest in acting, Catherine took notice. At the time, Catherine was a production designer in Hollywood who wanted to break into directing. She had worked on hit films like *Vanilla Sky* starring Tom Cruise, Penélope Cruz, and Cameron Diaz, and *Laurel Canyon* starring Christian Bale and Kate Beckinsale, but she wanted the chance to direct her own films. Catherine suggested that Nikki start writing as an outlet for expressing what she was going through. So Nikki did, and eventually, the pair decided to collaborate on a script that started out as a teen comedy about a good girl and a bad girl. But as more emotions and events from Nikki's imagination— and her real life experiences—went into the story, it turned into a very raw coming-of-age drama.

The script—which later turned into the movie *Thirteen*—delved into all the difficulties that typically come with adolescence, like feeling like you don't fit in at school, that your parents don't understand you, and the desire to grow up fast. Nikki described that time in her life in an interview on National Public Radio as ". . . a really confusing time. You don't know where you belong, you don't know where you're supposed to fit in." What Nikki probably didn't understand at the time was that this is something that *every* teenager feels every now and again. If you ever feel that way, there are lots of ways to express your emotions, like writing in a journal, talking to your friends, or playing a sport.

Nikki and Catherine's script involved two girls—Evie Zamora, a popular and beautiful junior high school girl—and Tracy Freeland—a straight-A student who comes from a broken home and wants to be more popular. Evie's bad influence completely corrupts eager-to-please Tracy, and both girls get more and more out of control, which eventually strains the relationship between Tracy and her mom.

Catherine and Nikki hammered out the script in only six days' time, which is totally unheard of for a Hollywood screenplay! Nikki had been on winter break from school and was spending time with Catherine at her home in Venice Beach. At the time, Nikki probably thought that working on the script together was just something fun that they were doing as a way for the two of them to bond and to help sort through Nikki's feelings. Little did she know what that "bonding" session would turn into!

After Nikki returned to school, Catherine went

to a party where she happened to meet a woman who was a therapist. The two got to talking about Nikki, and some of the hard times she was going through. As it turned out, the therapist had experiences of her own working with teens like Nikki, so she was immediately interested in the script that Catherine and Nikki had written together. She told Catherine to contact her husband, who was a movie producer.

The producer liked what he read, and hooked Catherine up with the Oscar-winning actress Holly Hunter. After reading the amazing script, Holly agreed to star in the film as Melanie Freeland, Tracy's mother. Evan Rachel Wood was cast as Tracy Freeland, and Nikki herself made her film debut as Evie! *Thirteen* was also the film debut of another cute up-and-coming actress: Vanessa Hudgens of *High School Musical* fame played a neighbor and school friend of Tracy's!

Even though she cowrote the script, and the movie was somewhat based on her own life, Nikki wasn't just handed the part. She auditioned along with four hundred other hopefuls. After all, Nikki's only acting experience at that point had been a school play in kindergarten, so she knew she had to prove herself. But Catherine was always there to support her. "Catherine was fighting for me all the way," Nikki told usatoday.com. Although Nikki ended up being cast as the bad girl, it was Tracy's character that she related to most in the movie.

Catherine and Nikki were so excited to actually see their movie on the big screen, but they had no idea what was in store for them! *Thirteen* screened at the Sundance Film Festival, the same place where Kristen Stewart got one of her first big breaks. Not only did the audience love it, but Catherine took home the Directoring Award! Critics raved about the movie, and about Nikki's part in it. *Rolling Stone* described Nikki as "strikingly good as Evie." Notoriously tough film critic Roger Ebert of the *Chicago Sun-Times* called Nikki's performance "a wild and seductive bad influence . . . persuasive and convincing . . . She has the gifts to do almost anything."

The critics weren't the only ones responding to Nikki's incredible debut role. Nikki was nominated for several awards for her work in *Thirteen*, too. She ended up winning an Independent Spirit Award for Best Debut Performance in 2004, as well as a Young Hollywood Award in the "One to Watch" category in 2003. Talk about the ultimate recognition!

Nikki was thrilled. She had made her acting debut to rave reviews. Plus, along the way, she was able to work out and express some of the feelings she had kept bottled up for so long. It was the ultimate win-win situation. But Nikki wasn't content just to rest on her successes. She wanted to continue acting, and she was determined to put all of her passion into being the best actress she could be. She hoped that her next role would bring her even half the success and honor her role in *Thirteen* did. Nikki had a lot to live up to, but she was ready for whatever was in store for her.

CHAPTER 8
The "Bad Girl"

After her success with *Thirteen*, Nikki Reed became pretty well-known in Hollywood for both her acting and writing abilities. Everyone was impressed that a teenager could both write and act in such a critically acclaimed film! Nikki described the success of *Thirteen* to the *Independent* (a British newspaper) as "shocking and really difficult in a lot of ways because it was so personal."

Even though Nikki's own life experiences were now out there for anyone to judge, she didn't regret working on *Thirteen*, even though she admits it greatly affected her parents, both positively and negatively. Nikki preferred to look on the bright side of everything—she had made a hit film, after all!—rather than feel regret for exposing herself and her problems with her family. Plus, working on the film helped her deal with a lot of issues, which ultimately was a positive thing for the young star. "I don't know where I would be, what I would be doing. And maybe I would be in a lot more trouble because I wouldn't have had to take responsibility. I mean, this misconception that I'm like this bad girl, it's just really funny because forcing me to move out and grow up really fast is what made me a good girl, is what forced me to pay bills and work and not [mess] around," Nikki told about.com. "I'm not [the bad girl], but that is what people think because I play that well."

After working on *Thirteen*, Nikki tried going back to high school, but found that she still didn't fit in. So she eventually took a test that allowed her to homeschool herself. She also moved out of her mom's house and became legally emancipated from her parents. This meant that she no longer was under their authority, nor were they responsible for her, even though she was a minor. It was a tough decision, but was the best thing for Nikki, because now she was responsible for taking care of herself. Plus, she always had Catherine to fall back on. After moving out, Nikki decided to throw herself headfirst into acting.

Nikki followed up her role in *Thirteen* with appearances in a pair of smaller independent films—*Man of God* and *American Gun*—in 2005. But 2005 was a big year for Nikki because that was also the year she decided to team up with Catherine again for Catherine's second directorial effort, another teen-centered flick called *Lords of Dogtown*. Everyone wondered: Could the talented twosome strike gold twice?

Nikki thought so, and she was thrilled to work with Catherine again. In an interview with teenhollywood.com, Nikki admitted how much working with Catherine meant to her: "Everything that she is and is continuing to do, I aspire to be and do one day. Hopefully I'll follow in those footsteps." But it wasn't just Catherine that Nikki responded to—she also really loved the script!

The gritty biographical film was about skateboarding culture in the 1970s. It told the true story of a group of surfers-turned-skaters from the Venice Beach area of Southern California who formed a skating team called the "Z-Boys," after the Zephyr Surf Shop, the local surf shop that agreed to sponsor the team. The teens' inventive, acrobatic stunts came to redefine skateboarding. The movie was spun off of a 2001 documentary called *Dogtown and Z-Boys*, which was written and directed by skateboarding legend and original Z-Boy, Stacy Peralta. At nineteen, he was the highest-ranked professional skateboarder in the world. His documentary won both the Audience Award and Documentary Directing Award at Sundance. Catherine's film, *Lords of Dogtown*, chronicles the events leading to the creation of skateboarding as an extreme sport. Two things happened in Venice, California, in the mid-1970s that started it all.

First, there was a severe drought in Los Angeles that prompted the government to prohibit people from filling their swimming pools. The empty pools had deep bowls surrounded by sloped interiors—the perfect surface for boarding.

Second, polyurethane wheels—which were very soft and gripped the ground—came onto the skateboarding scene. Suddenly, you could ride a skateboard in a way you never could before.

The film featured several young stars, including Emile Hirsch (who also starred with Kristen Stewart in *Into the Wild*!) and the late, great Heath Ledger. Michael Angarano, Kristen's future boyfriend, also starred. In the film, Nikki plays the character of Kathy Alva, sister to skater Tony Alva, one of the Z-Boys. She was also the love interest of Tony's two skater friends, Stacy and Jay.

Although *Lords of Dogtown* did not receive the level of acclaim that *Thirteen* did, Nikki had a blast making the film. Hanging out on the set with a bunch of hot boarding dudes was totally fun. She even learned to skateboard, too! Plus, she had an amazing time working with Catherine again.

Nikki's next appearance was on the popular FOX series *The O.C.*, which followed the lives of a group of people living in an upper-class neighborhood in Newport Beach, Orange County (also known simply as the O.C.), California. (Fellow *Twilight* cast members Jackson Rathbone and Cam Gigandet also appeared on the show.) *The O.C.* ran for four seasons, from 2003–2007. For six episodes in 2006, Nikki played the character of Sadie Campbell, a girl who catches the eye of Ryan Atwood, the show's main character who, similar to Nikki, is a reformed wild child.

Nikki loved working on independent films, so it was a surprise to some people that she accepted a role on a television series. Nikki admits she was reluctant at first, but eventually figured out that it was all about the experience. "I guess I lost the battle that I was having with my team, which was that new experiences and change [are] not . . . bad thing[s]," she told zap2it.com. Plus, it didn't hurt that at the time, *The O.C.* was one of the hottest shows on television!

Nikki followed up her work on *The O.C.* with two more turns as the teen "bad girl"—first, as young temptress Minerva "Mini" Droggs in the 2006 film *Mini's First Time* and then as femme fatale Shay Bettencourt in *Cherry Crush* in 2007.

After that, Nikki turned back to television and filmed a pilot for a new show on the CW called *Reaper*. *Reaper* was about a young man named Sam Oliver who becomes a bounty hunter for the devil. His job is basically to recapture the souls that have escaped from hell. Nikki was cast as Andi Prendergast, Sam's beautiful love interest. But before the pilot aired, her role was recast with another actress, Missy Peregrym, who had just come off a recurring role in the popular NBC series *Heroes*.

Nikki didn't let that minor setback bother her, and instead, looked forward to her next role in the 2008 independent film *Familiar Strangers*. This quirky comedy was about a family that gets together for the long Thanksgiving weekend. The oldest son, Brian, left years before to pursue his own career rather than take over the family business.

Nikki played the character of Allison, a family friend who has always secretly liked Brian and helps him discover the appreciation and love he has for his family. Her character was a lot more lighthearted in this movie and showcased Nikki's versatility as an actress.

But it was her prowess at playing the bad girl that helped her land her next role—the biggest role of her young life!

CHAPTER 9
It's *Rocket Science*

Adorable Anna Kendrick's story begins on August 9, 1985, when she was born in Portland, Maine.

Unlike her *Twilight* costars, Anna actually began her acting career in the theater. "[I was] one of those hyperactive kids who wanted to jump around and sing and dance and scream and be on stage," she told backstage.com. Her first onstage appearance was when she was only six years old. She played Tessie in a community theater production of *Annie*. A few years later she appeared in a production of *Gypsy* at the Maine State Music Theatre.

"My parents were really, really cool about supporting what I wanted to do at a really young age," Anna told MTV.com. "I think I was about ten when I caught the [acting] bug. They would drive me down to New York if there were auditions." Her brother, Michael Cooke Kendrick, is two years older and is an actor as well.

At the age of eleven, Anna signed on with agent Kim Matuka, founder of Online Talent Group, a New York–based theatrical management company.

Anna's passion turned to reality when she won her first real role! In 1998, at the age of twelve, she was cast in a Broadway musical called *High Society*. This play tells the story of a snooty socialite named Tracy Lord who is set to marry an equally snobby executive when her ex-husband shows up and disrupts everything. Anna played Tracy's precocious younger sister Dinah. The show ran from April to August.

Anna wowed the New York theater critics and was subsequently nominated for several theater awards, including Broadway's highest honor—a Tony Award for Best Featured Actress in a Musical. She was the second youngest actress ever to receive such recognition! At age twelve, Anna was already a bona fide star!

She was also nominated for a Drama Desk Award (which recognizes excellence in all New York theaters, not just Broadway productions) and a Theater World

Award (which recognizes a debut performance either on or off-Broadway), the latter of which she won!

Of course the recognition and nominations were exciting for Anna, but just being onstage performing was thrilling enough. "I think as a child actor the experience is always incredible—but very difficult," she said to backstage.com. "But I don't think anybody would trade it, because it's so unique and so special. It is isolating, especially in my case; there were no other kids in the show. And it was sort of overwhelming, but some of the actors and actresses in that were so great to me . . . and really helped me feel like I was part of the show."

After the show wrapped, Anna didn't try for another big role right away. Instead, she did some Broadway workshops, including *Jane Eyre* and *The Little Princess*, and according to Anna, "did the normal adolescent thing." For Anna, that meant going to school at Deering High School in Portland and just hanging out with friends. "I'm really glad I got to have that experience," she told backstage.com.

But Anna wasn't done with the Broadway spotlight quite yet. She graduated high school early, and in

March 2003, she went to work in the New York City Opera's brief off-Broadway revival of *A Little Night Music* from famed composer Stephen Sondheim. Set in Sweden, the musical is about the romantic relationships between several couples who all come together one summer night at a country estate. Anna's character, Fredrika Armfeldt, is the thirteen-year-old daughter of the female lead character, Desirée Armfeldt. "Send in the Clowns," sung by Desirée, is the musical's most well-known song.

Up to that point, Anna hadn't had much interest in branching out from Broadway. But once other acting offers starting rolling in, she began to consider that maybe she could be a successful actress outside of Broadway, too. The offers turned out to be too tempting for Anna to turn down, so she moved to Los Angeles and, later in 2003, made her film debut in an independent project called *Camp*. The setting of this well-received musical comedy is an upstate New York performing arts summer camp. Anna played the character of Fritzi Wagner, a hilarious ticking time-bomb who tries to undermine Jill, the camp's prima donna, and her many successes.

Anna had a lot of fun playing a girl with some stalker-like habits! "She's creepy," Anna told *USA Today*. "There were definitely some days where I didn't want to wear the huge sweatshirt and the grease they put in my hair, especially the first day when it was like 100 degrees and everybody else was complaining—until they saw me with grease dripping down my face and massive black eyeliner going everywhere."

Anna's talent definitely translated from Broadway to the big screen. The movie received very positive reviews, including one from *Rolling Stone*, which called Anna "terrific." And *Film Comment* magazine thunderously applauded her "dazzling . . . transformation from subservient follower to take-no-prisoners diva." Even better, *Camp* was nominated for the Grand Jury Prize at the 2003 Sundance Film Festival, and Anna herself was nominated for Best Debut Performance at the 2004 Independent Spirit Awards! Anna had had a taste of success, and she wanted more. She set out to audition for—and hopefully land—more film roles.

And land them she did! Anna's next film role

came in 2007 when she played the character of Ginny Ryerson in a coming-of-age indie film titled *Rocket Science*. In the movie, Ginny is the talented, fast-talking leader of a high school debate team. Ambitious but manipulative, she recruits a stuttering student to be her partner on the team—only to leave the school at a later date and join a rival school's debate team where she simultaneously wins the competition while watching her former partner crash and burn.

Although she won the part during a conventional audition, little did Anna know that writer/director Jeffrey Blitz had her pegged as Ginny the second he saw her! "I wrote down in my notebook when Anna first came in, 'Anna Kendrick is Ginny Ryerson,'" he told backstage.com. "I just knew it."

In fact, later during rehearsals, Jeff asked the actors to do some free-association writing as their characters. "Jeff suggested that I seek therapy because what I had written was so frighteningly in tune with the character," Anna laughingly told teenhollywood.com.

It was definitely a great role for Anna, but proved to be a lot tougher than she thought. In particular, playing a debate speaker proved to be challenging because Anna had to deliver lines from the movie's debate scenes at a mile-a-minute pace and with accuracy and confidence, just like a real debate. "I thought I was a fast talker naturally," she told *Variety*. "And then we saw this video of a national collegiate championship, and I thought, 'I can't do this. What have I gotten myself into?'"

The pressure was definitely on for the young actress. One slipup would wreck the whole scene—and with indie films, time and money are always in short supply! "[I was] sweating buckets with every take . . . I would really, really try to get it right, because I knew we had a tight schedule. When I would mess up, the cursing that would follow was really severe," Anna joked to MTV.com.

But Anna nailed it. The movie captivated the audience at its Sundance screening and was nominated for the Grand Jury Prize, even though it didn't win. However, writer/director Jeffrey Blitz took home the Directing Award that year at Sundance—which was, incidentally, presented to him by none other than *Twilight* director

Catherine Hardwicke! Plus, the critics loved the movie, and applauded Anna's stellar performance. *Variety* praised Anna (and her costar, Nicholas D'Agosto) for their mastery of the debate technique known as "spreading," which is the rapid-fire delivery of one side of a debate argument. Anna must have been pretty pleased—that was the one thing she really struggled with during the filming! "[It] was really nerve-wracking and difficult," Anna told MTV.com. "Everybody would ask me how I learned to do it. And I never really had a clear answer. It was just a matter of trying it again and again and, you know, spitting it out." Anna, along with her costar, Nicholas D'Agosto, was also applauded by *Variety* for the "fierce, meticulous concentration [brought to their] delightfully cocky performances as Type A overachievers." Critic Roger Ebert of the *Chicago Sun-Times* predicted Anna was "early in what promise[s] to be [a] considerable [career]. Kendrick can make you like her even when you shouldn't." Plus, Anna was once again nominated for an Independent Spirit Award for Best Supporting Female, but unfortunately didn't win. She did, however, get named to *Variety*'s 2007 list of "10 Actors to Watch"—further proof that the entertainment industry was taking notice!

Anna could have rested on her laurels, but she chose not to. In fact, she had two more films slated for 2007—and they couldn't have been more different! In the indie thriller *Elsewhere*, Anna had her first leading role as Sarah, a straight-A, straitlaced teenager whose trouble-making best friend Jillian goes missing from the girls' small hometown in Indiana after recklessly trying to meet men online. It was a heavy role, but Anna nailed it with her usual grace.

After that, she went the complete opposite route, and acted in a comedic film called *The Marc Pease Experience*. Anna played high school senior and musical theater fanatic Meg Brickman who has a romantic relationship with the title character, a twenty-eight-year-old man who can't quite leave behind his "glory days" as the star of his high school's musicals. The movie also starred funnyman Ben Stiller. "That was really fun; I got to smooch both of them," she told backstage.com.

It was the perfect role for the Broadway veteran. Anna got to show off her musical theater background by singing a cappella opposite Ben, who played Mr. Gribble, Marc's former theater teacher and mentor.

"The very first thing that I shot was doing vocal warm-ups with Ben's character. He's my music teacher . . . We had to do a-capella vocal warm-ups, just scales on whatever syllable he felt like saying. He just kept going and improving. It was like poobah, and peebo and moopie. Whatever he'd say, I'd have to sing that. Everybody thought it was so funny but I'm like 'I'm going to kill you,'" she laughingly told teenhollywood.com.

But Anna held her own brilliantly beside the hilarious comedic actor. "Every time we would cut, people would be so impressed that I wasn't breaking [up] or laughing," Kendrick told *Variety*. "I was like, 'If I could stop feeling like I was about to throw up, it would occur to me to laugh.'"

Anna was truly on her way to stardom! She'd gone from Broadway, where she was well-known in theater circles but not to the general public, to starring opposite a hugely popular comedian like

Ben Stiller in just a few years. She probably thought that it couldn't get much better than that. Until a role came along for a movie that would put her on the map.

CHAPTER 10

The Actress-Singer-Dancer-Model-Figure Skater

The beautiful Christian Marie Serratos was born on September 21, 1990, in Pasadena, California, but she was actually raised in the San Fernando Valley (or, simply, "the Valley") in Los Angeles.

Growing up, Christian juggled a lot of activities, but she loved all of them and didn't mind having such a busy schedule. She was an active and athletic child who started taking figure skating lessons when she was only three years old. She was a really talented figure skater and competed in the sport for ten years. There was even a time when her coaches were talking about training her for the Olympics! Christian says that the competitive spirit she learned as a skater has actually helped her a lot as an actress.

On top of that, Christian is also a dancer trained in ballet, tap, and jazz. "I started . . . when I was really little," she told *Girls' Life*. "You know how the little girl wants to put on the tutu and do ballet. So I did that, and the singing, I'd love to start up with that again. And acting kind of fell into my lap, and I ended up absolutely loving it."

Yup, you heard right—Christian is also a talented singer and musician, and has been since childhood! She says on her official MySpace page, "I would never give up my acting, but I can't even begin to tell you how passionate I am about my music." In fact, she even has an original song—"Why Are Boys Like That"—on her official MySpace music page.

As far as musical influences, Christian names Queen, 4 Non Blondes/Linda Perry, Fiona Apple, Christina Aguilera, Regina Spektor, Flyleaf, Sia Furler, Mindless Self Indulgence, and Roisin Murphy as some of her favorites. Christian loves writing her own music, too. She told teenhollywood.com, "I started off writing music. I don't think I ever wanted to be a singer. I think I just wanted to write. But, if I did end up doing anything with my music, I wanted to be singing it. And then, I realized I wasn't so bad. Then, it was just practice and that competitiveness I've got." Unlike Kristen, Christian is definitely interested in pursuing music professionally. "[But] it will probably be once *Twilight* is done, just 'cause it's been so time consuming," she told teenhollywood.com.

Christian's competitiveness is a personality trait she mentions often in interviews. Obviously it helped during her figure skating years—but it also rears its head when she's just hanging out playing video games! "I absolutely do not have the skills for Guitar Hero, but don't even think I'm not going to talk trash when I play. Even when I'm losing, I will continue to talk trash. Every time my friend Brittany and I pick up Guitar Hero, I'm like, 'Are you ready to go down again?' And she just laughs because she knows she will kick my butt. I'm on medium right now, but I pass just barely by the skin of my teeth," Christian laughingly told *Girls' Life*. This competitive streak will definitely help her out as she tries for more acting roles in the future.

So how did the young talent get her start as an actress, anyway? Christian's unique good looks got her accepted as a model at the Ford Modeling Agency, but she quickly realized she preferred acting over modeling when she got involved with the agency's theatrical acting division. Plus, as a child, Christian would entertain her family by reenacting television shows for them in the Serratos family living room, so it was only natural that acting would appeal to her!

Christian's first acting job was an independent short film in 2004 called *Mrs. Marshall* in which she played Jillian Marshall, the daughter of the title character. The movie, about an odd boy who develops a painful crush on a housewife (Mrs. Marshall) across the street, premiered at the famous Cannes Film Festival in France, but was never picked up for distribution. But with the confidence she gained by booking that role, Christian forged ahead with other auditions and soon was lucky enough to get her big break as an actress on one of the best channels for kids—Nickelodeon! She snagged the recurring role of Suzie Crabgrass in the live action teen sitcom *Ned's Declassified School Survival Guide.* The series aired on Nickelodeon from September 2004 until June 2007, and Christian appeared in forty-four episodes.

Ned's Declassified School Survival Guide takes

place at a fictional school called the James K. Polk Middle School. The storyline revolves around three main characters who are best friends trying to navigate their way through middle school. The title character of Ned Bigby, played by Devon Werkheiser, created the "survival guide" that the show is named for after accidentally walking into the girls' bathroom in kindergarten. Talk about embarrassing!

Ned's two best friends on the show are volleyball jock Jennifer Ann Mosely, or "Moze," played by actress Lindsey Shaw, and computer geek Simon Nelson Cook, or "Cookie," played by actor Dan Curtis Lee.

Christian's character Suzie had been Ned's crush since he was eight years old. In the third and final season of the series, the two finally start dating. But toward the end of the season, Suzie and Ned break up, and Ned begins dating his long-time best friend Moze, while Suzie ends up with the school bully.

Christian's acting skills and natural charm earned her a Young Artist Award nomination in 2008 in the category of Best Performance in a TV Series—Recurring Young Actress. She lost to Erin Sanders, who plays the character Quinn Pensky on another Nick teen show—*Zoey 101*.

Christian also appeared in a 2006 Disney Channel original movie called *Cow Belles*. The movie starred sisters Alyson and Amanda Michalka—better known as the rock duo Aly & AJ—as spoiled and irresponsible teens who are ordered by their father to straighten up. He puts them in charge of the family business—a dairy operation—while he goes out of town. Of course everything falls apart on the sisters' watch, including the theft of all the company's money from its bank account, and it's up to the girls to save the day. In the movie, Christian played the character Heather Perez, a good friend of the sisters whose father works at the dairy.

On top of all that, Christian did some guest appearances on a handful of popular television shows. Those appearances included *Zoey 101* (in 2005), *7th Heaven* (in 2006), and *Hannah Montana* (in 2007). On *Zoey 101*, the Nickelodeon teen show starring Britney Spears's little sister Jamie Lynn, Christian appeared as a student in a first season episode called "School Dance." On *Hannah Montana*, the smash

Disney Channel hit starring Miley Cyrus, Christian appeared briefly as a classmate named Alexa in a first season episode called "The Idol Side of Me." And on *7th Heaven*, she appeared as a receptionist in an episode titled "Broken Hearts and Promises."

With lots of small guest appearances under her belt and her recurring role in *Ned's Declassified* wrapping up in 2007, Christian was probably eager to find another project. Never in her wildest dreams could she have guessed what was in store for her next!

CHAPTER 11

Becoming Bella

Summit Entertainment, the fledgling movie company that produced *Twilight*, is not unlike the vampire character of Edward Cullen: They were both just waiting for the right thing to come along. As every diehard Twilighter knows, in Edward's case, it was, of course, his soul mate Bella. In Summit's case, it was the right project that would get them the attention of the larger studios and, as a result, the funding they needed to turn their company into a money-making machine. That much-needed project turned out to be *Twilight*, but it was not their movie to make—at least not at first.

One of the biggest movie studios in Hollywood, Paramount Pictures, originally had the movie rights for the first book in Stephenie Meyer's series. In 2006, the studio let the rights expire, which is not uncommon when studios option film rights.

But, wow, what a big mistake that turned out to be!

When the executives at Summit found out the rights to *Twilight* were once again available, they did some research. They noted that the sales of the books were, of course, solid. But what *really* stood out to them was the series' very extensive online fan base. There were a whole lot of young girls following the book and talking about it on blogs. That planted the seed that maybe there was more to the series than the book sales alone suggested, and they decided to see if they could turn the first book in the series, *Twilight*, into a movie.

But first they had to convince *Twilight* author Stephenie Meyer that they were the right partner to make the movie. Other companies had tried this before, and failed. One time, Stephenie actually read (and turned down) a version of a script that turned Bella into a track star! In theory, Stephenie was okay with the idea of turning her book into a film. But she felt that some of the scenes in the movie should match the scenes from the book exactly, in order to stay true to the book. One of those scenes was the meadow scene—the point in the movie where Edward shows Bella that, as a vampire, he sparkles in the sun.

Before Summit, "there was another script," Stephenie told *MediaBlvd* magazine. "They could have filmed it and not called it *Twilight* because it had nothing to do with the book, and that's kind of frightening. When Summit came into the picture, they were so open to letting us make the rules for them, like, 'OK, Bella cannot be a track star. Bella cannot have a gun or night vision goggles. And, no jet skis. Are you okay with that?' And, they were so cool!"

Summit's executives were respectful of Stephenie's desire to make a film that truly represented the world, characters, and storyline she had so lovingly created. So they even included language in their contract with her that stated "no vampire character will be depicted with canine or incisor teeth longer or more pronounced than may be found in human beings." Imagine if every movie contract included a clause like this! Needless to say, Stephenie was sold, and after that things started moving quickly.

Summit hired Nikki's mentor and friend, Catherine Hardwicke, to direct, and together she and screenwriter Melissa Rosenberg, who also wrote the 2006 dance drama *Step Up* and produced and cowrote for *The O.C.,* wrote a first draft of the script in only six weeks.

Melissa was very interested in exploring the book's characters, especially Bella. ". . . I was really intrigued by Bella, who is really the everygirl brought into this new world. She was someone I wanted to see more of and develop," she told the *Los Angeles Times* blog. So of course the next daunting task was to cast the characters—starting with Bella.

Because the books had such a huge online fan base, Catherine knew her casting choices would be closely monitored and that her every move would be scrutinized. Twilighters love these books, and she knew they would be very vocal about whether they considered her casting choices to be bad or good. She especially knew that casting the role of Bella would be pivotal. The actress who won the role would have to be able to carry the film. Considering Bella is the first and only creature to have caught the attention of the century-old heartthrob Edward, the actress Catherine chose would have to be pretty special!

Catherine also felt it was important to cast an actual teenager to play Bella—which only added to the complexity of the casting, because the actress also had to be mature enough to convey Bella's emotional depth.

As luck would have it, Catherine found her Bella fairly quickly. She had just seen Kristen Stewart as the soulful musician Tracy Tatro in *Into the Wild* and "her mixture of innocence and longing just knocked me out," Catherine told *Entertainment Weekly*. Plus, it didn't hurt that Kristen's costar, Emile Hirsch, whom Catherine had worked with in *Lords of Dogtown*, gave the young actress his full endorsement.

At the time of casting, Kristen was shooting the movie *Adventureland* in Pittsburgh. So Catherine took a red-eye flight there and did an impromptu screen test with her. What she saw must have impressed her, because Kristen won the role on the spot after nailing a four-hour audition! "She'd been shooting all night, but she learned her lines on the spot," Hardwicke told *Entertainment Weekly*. "She danced on the bed and chased pigeons in the park. I was captivated."

Kristen probably didn't know what she was getting herself into at the time. She even admits that she had not read the books prior to her audition. "I don't know if I was living under a big boulder rock," she admitted to the capacity crowd at Comic-Con. "But I hadn't heard of the book[s] until Catherine came to me." One reason for that could have been that, as a fan of classic literature, Kristen actually prefers to go to used bookstores.

Believe it or not, Kristen's first impression of *Twilight* wasn't a positive one! "I read a synopsis of the story *before* I read the script or the book—and I hated it," she admitted to the *Los Angeles Times* blog. "The synopsis made Bella so weak, as though the only reason she wanted to be with Edward was because he was the most beautiful thing she had ever seen, because he could take care of her, because she didn't have to be brave because he could be brave for her." In Kristen's opinion, the synopsis—which was only a summary of the movie—presented young love in a way that seemed not only unrealistic, but also unachievable. It wasn't a message that Kristen was comfortable spreading to young girls. But once she read the actual script, she changed her mind, because there was a lot more detail and insight into the characters. Kristen liked the direction that Melissa took Bella in the script, and she was excited to bring her to life on the big screen!

Considering Kristen's past roles were mostly smaller independent films, some *Twilight* fans might wonder why she would accept a role in a movie that had a good chance of becoming a mainstream blockbuster franchise, considering the book's track record with fans. ". . . I don't think in terms of how big the movies are going to be or if it's Hollywood or independent," Kristen responded to scifi.com. "I just want to work with the people that inspire me, and I want to be the characters that I feel responsible for . . . I can only do films that I feel very much compelled to do." Plus, Kristen had no idea that the movie would turn out to be as wildly popular as it was. "I figured it was a little cult vampire movie with a built-in fan base," she told *Entertainment Weekly*.

"What I love about the story is that it's about a very logical, pragmatic girl who you think would never get swept into something that has this bizarre power."

This was Kristen's first time playing the role of a teenage girl experiencing those fierce, almost uncontrollable longings that come with a first love. Longings that are especially fierce because they're directed toward someone a little bit dangerous—a bad boy. After all, Edward had to fight all his instincts not to kill Bella! Kristen was excited to explore that essential aspect of the story.

Throughout her career, Kristen has proven that she is a thoughtful actress who cares a lot about the characters she plays and how she will portray them. In this case, figuring out how to play the part of Bella was more demanding than actually scoring the role itself! "The only thing I could bring to Bella was to be myself," Kristen said in an interview with *Entertainment Weekly*. "She's an honest, up-front, seemingly logical girl. She's alone but not lonely." Luckily, being a teenage girl herself, Kristen didn't find it hard to identify with the character. "Bella is sort of easy for every girl to relate to," she told *Access*

Hollywood. "You feel like you are her when you're reading the book. It's a total vicarious experience—she really encompasses the best fundamental female qualities. She's a little insecure but she compensates, she likes herself and she trusts herself."

It might be hard to see Bella as a "typical teen"—after all, she does have to ward off bloodthirsty vampires on an almost daily basis—but Stephenie Meyer doesn't think so. "I think she's more of a typical teen than people give her credit for," Stephenie said to *MediaBlvd* magazine. "She's a little more withdrawn and she's quieter . . . [But] there's a lot of people who are just quieter, and who aren't having the Prada lifestyle, and who don't go to a special school in New York, where everyone's rich and fabulous."

Kristen and Catherine had many conversations about how strong the character of Bella actually is—a definite change of heart for Kristen, who early on thought Bella was very weak. "A lot of people disagree with [thinking she's strong], because she gives up some control. But I think it takes a lot of courage to give up that control," Kristen explained to the *Star-*

Ledger. "It's a really striking story, because it's just so fundamental. What do we live for? . . . [and] you have to say, 'For someone else, for companionship.' And the story is about what you sacrifice for that."

But ultimately, what may have really drawn Kristen to the role was the relationship between her character and the heartbreakingly handsome Edward Cullen. She told the *Los Angeles Times* blog: "You see that the power balance between Edward and Bella is actually really skewed and more interesting. We have a girl who is insanely naive and has no idea what she's getting into, yet she trusts herself enough to put stock in what she feels and gives up the power to him. And he's afraid and tortured and entirely conflicted, whereas she's not. She becomes the assertive force in the relationship. It's an ambitious thing to try to portray the ultimate love story, and I thought it would be a good project."

Stephenie Meyer was incredibly happy with the casting of Kristen as Bella, and why wouldn't she be? Kristen wowed audiences as the gentle but strong Bella. In fact, *Rolling Stone's* review of the movie gave big props to Kristen, who "brings just the right blend of ferocity and feeling to the role of Bella Swan." Stephenie even admits that Kristen is an ideal actress for the vision of Bella she had in her head. "Kristen does a version of Bella that's very strong," she told *USA Today.* "And you can see that what she's doing is maturely thought out. In a lot of ways she's a little bit impetuous, but you get the sense that she's very adult about what she's doing. She comes across as a girl who's very serious and who happens to know what she wants."

Another thing Kristen knew she wanted—Rob Pattinson as Edward. Kristen knew he was the perfect choice for the role from the moment she met him. Looks like she was right!

CHAPTER 12
Vampire Sisters and School Chums

Twilight fans who devoured the books might be a little shocked to know this about the movie's leading ladies: Christian Serratos was the only girl who was familiar with the books prior to the auditions! In fact, none of the other actresses had even heard of the books, which is surprising, considering how popular Stephenie Meyer's series was before the first movie even hit theaters.

But not being familiar with the books didn't stop Ashley, Nikki, and Anna from bringing something to their auditions that made Catherine think—*she's the one!*

Alice Cullen was one of the first characters cast after Bella and Edward. Ashley said it was a long process—she actually went through four months of auditions! Ashley really had no idea what she was getting herself into in the beginning. Her management didn't give her a lot of information up front about the audition when they called her about it—other than it was for a book series that could turn into a few films. They definitely didn't tell her that there was a possibility *Twilight* could turn into something huge. So their advice to the young star was to the point: You need to do a good job. Don't mess up.

"I really didn't know what a big deal it was, but I knew it was something," Ashley told *MediaBlvd* magazine. "I had no idea what was going on. There was no script. There was no breakdown (detailed character descriptions). So, I postponed my meeting for two days, and read the entire first book. And then, I went in and auditioned and, surprisingly enough, I got a callback and was like, 'Oh, my God, this is great!'"

Ashley may not have known what she was getting herself into after that first phone call with her agent, but after reading *Twilight*, she completely understood why the series was so popular. "I can relate with the fans as far as how they're in love with the Edward character, because he's literally this perfect being and I totally get it. It's so funny working with all these people and seeing them in real life. I'm just as big a fan of Stephenie [Meyer] and of the books as anybody else. I just happened to get the opportunity to portray Alice," she told *Vanity Fair*.

Ashley met a couple of times with Catherine Hardwicke, and recognizing her talent, Catherine was determined not to let Ashley go. She brought her back in several times to audition for the part of Alice. Ashley gave it her all, and thought her auditions went really well. But it was nearing Christmas of 2007, and Ashley still hadn't heard anything about the part, even though filming was scheduled to start in February 2008. She went back home to Florida to spend the holiday with her family.

At that point, Ashley really believed she didn't get the part, and she was totally bummed about it. "I was upset about it. I cried about it. It was just one of those parts where I was like, 'This is *my* part!' There are some parts where you're just like, 'This is my part, and nobody can do a better job,' and that was this," she explained to *MediaBlvd* magazine.

So when Ashley finally got the call at home in Florida saying she'd won the role of Alice Cullen, she was beyond excited—and cried all over again, this time for a happy reason! And when she told her parents, they cried, too. "They were so excited. It was cute. It was one of those monumental [moments] in your life," she said to *MediaBlvd* magazine. Ashley's parents had always been supportive of her, so it's not surprising that they were so emotional about what they (correctly) assumed could become her breakout role.

So why did Ashley get the part, besides her obvious acting talent? She said that one of the most significant things that worked in her favor was that she fit the description of the character, minus the height. In the book, Alice is described as four feet eleven inches, but Ashley is five feet five inches. It was probably a pretty funny situation for Ashley, who had been told when she was younger that she was too short to be a model. Now the situation was reversed—she was technically too tall! But luckily, this time it was an easy fix—Ashley just had to wear flats! One other thing that almost worked against her was the lack of film roles on her résumé. In the end, Catherine's belief in her talent won out, and the director decided to take a chance on her.

Ashley knew she was lucky to get the role—in more ways than one! Her casting didn't cause nearly as much fan backlash as the others, particularly Rob Pattinson's casting. She said that the fans' feedback was relatively gentle by comparison. "Even the negative responses weren't like, 'We hate her!' They were more like, 'Oh, she's too tall' or 'Her hair is too long.' It wasn't like, 'She's awful, she could never play Alice!' So I am very thankful. It's rough, and some of the people weren't so lucky," Ashley told film.com.

One person whose reaction to Ashley was immediately positive? Stephenie Meyer herself. "[The] one that really jumped out was Ashley Greene as Alice. I saw a picture of her and just thought, 'You found Alice! Oh my gosh!'" Stephenie told the *Los Angeles Times* blog.

Twilight fans and Ashley have one thing in common—they both love Alice! And it's easy to see why—she's sweet, bubbly, kind, a great sister, and a fantastic friend. Oh, and she has an awesome superpower! "She's so lovable. [S]he's just extremely happy to be alive . . . and to have a family who loves her. And she's kind of out for the better good, even though she is a vampire, of other people in her family. And she's just upbeat and happy, and then she has this [totally cool] power of being able to see the future. I don't think that hurts either," Ashley told about.com about why she thought her character was so popular with fans.

When an actor brings a character to life in a movie, it certainly helps to have some real-life experience to draw from. But, of course, in this case, Ashley didn't know any vampires to talk to about proper vampire behavior! But she wasn't too worried. She knew there were plenty of other ways for her to truly become Alice. "Going through hair and makeup doesn't hurt. Having someone say they're going to make you look as good as possible doesn't hurt. And having someone dress you doesn't hurt. Plus having . . . that movie magic we rely on. I didn't really think about it that way though. The character Alice doesn't look at things and say, 'I'm better, I'm superior.' She's just happy to be there, happy to be alive. So I focused more on that," she told film.com. And, given her very close relationships with her mom, dad, and older brother, Joe, it was probably very easy for Ashley to play the part of someone as loving as Alice.

Of course, Alice's amazing power—foreseeing the future—was definitely not something Ashley had any experience with. In order to play the part of her character accurately, Ashley turned to a number of different sources to learn about psychic abilities. She watched movies like *The Fifth Element*, read books and poetry, and researched a lot online.

Exploring her relationship with her soul mate, Jasper, was a big part of Ashley's character study, too. After all, Alice and Jasper have been a happy couple for many years—and Ashley and Jackson Rathbone, who stars as Jasper, had only just met when filming began! "The great thing about Jasper and Alice's relationship is that it's very mental too, so we don't even really have to touch the whole film. It's a very mental, deep connection. Jackson and I aren't gonna have that deep connection in three months, but [our characters] don't even need to speak. We know each other inside and out, and we are extremely protective of each other. The only time we really touch is when it's a crucial moment in the film, or if I'm seeing a vision and he's worried about me," Ashley explained to MTV.com.

Of course one of the best parts of playing Alice was her extensive wardrobe! In *Twilight*, Alice is a total fashionista—she loves to shop for clothes, for herself *and* for Bella! Ashley definitely didn't mind that aspect of her role. "I have the biggest wardrobe of everyone here," Ashley told MTV.com. "They have pulled so much stuff for me. I've had a lot of fittings, and we're making this fairy-tale thing kind of modern but still going back to the 1920s. It's a difficult wardrobe to do." One part of Alice's "wardrobe"—or any of the Cullen vampires—that wasn't required? Fangs. And Ashley admitted to feeling a little bit of disappointment with that particular aspect of the otherwise awesome *Twilight* vampire universe. Ashley would have loved to have worn fangs, and who can blame her? Not exactly a fashion choice you can make in everyday life!

And though she did an amazing job of bringing the character of Alice to life, who do you think Ashley would choose to be if she could play a different character? Sweet Ashley would play Victoria! "I like her role a lot. She's ferocious, and she's in it to win it . . . It's like my character's spunky and fun and good-hearted, and [Victoria]'s just evil," Ashley told MTV.com.

After Ashley signed on to play Alice, the next step was casting the character of Rosalie, who is known for being incredibly beautiful but also very cold. Catherine would have to find a gorgeous actress who could also nail down Rosalie's hostile side. So, of course, one person who came to mind was her friend and *Thirteen* star, Nikki Reed. Months before filming began, Nikki received a phone call about the part of Rosalie. At that point, much like Ashley, she didn't really understand just how popular *Twilight* was with its fans, primarily because she hadn't read the books. But that all changed when she knew she was going to be auditioning for Rosalie's part. "[T]here was very little hype about the idea, at least in my world. I hadn't heard of the books, to be perfectly honest. I read the three books that were available . . . [because] the rest of [the cast] who wanted to give the movie a deeper feel had to read [them]. Rosalie's character doesn't really get fleshed out until the third book, so I had to read it to know where she was coming from and to make her more than just background," Nikki told *Vanity Fair*.

Catherine knew Nikki would be perfect for the role—and she was right. "Rosalie Cullen is, even Stephenie Meyer says, quite a [nasty girl]. Nikki can pull that off! Nikki is just like such a little [tough chick]. She said, 'Catherine, you want me to play the character that everyone's going to hate because everyone wants Edward and Bella to be together but Rosalie doesn't? I'm fine with that!' She's so feisty and funny," Catherine told the *Los Angeles Times* blog. Once again, Nikki was cast as the "bad girl," but she didn't mind one bit!

But the fans certainly minded! Aside from Edward and Bella, the Twilighters were especially vocal about the casting of dark-haired, dark-skinned Nikki as the blonde and pale Rosalie. And that put a lot of additional pressure on the young actress.

KRISTEN, **ANNA,** and **NIKKI** look glam and gorgeous.

GLAMOROUS GIRLS

KRISTEN and **ROB PATTINSON** have great chemistry— on-screen and off!

KRISTEN poses with costars at the *ADVENTURELAND* premiere in L.A.

RED CARPET READY

ASHLEY with her costars **RACHELLE LEFEVRE** and **KELLAN LUTZ** at the *TWILIGHT* DVD launch party

CAST
SNAPSHOTS

CHRISTIAN looking angelic in white at a premiere

NIKKI, PETER FACINELLI, and JENNIE GARTH look stunning in black and white on the red carpet.

ANNA KENDRICK

ANNA rocking a trendy handband and LBD

ANNA poses with **LANCE BASS** on the red carpet.

CHRISTIAN with *TWILIGHT* director **CATHERINE HARDWICKE**

CHRISTIAN shows off some dangly earrings and a gorgeous smile.

CHRISTIAN SERRATOS

ASHLEY and *90210* star JESSICA LOWNDES look cute in blue jeans at an event in L.A.

ASHLEY with her costar and on-screen brother JACKSON RATHBONE

ASHLEY
GREENE

ASHLEY looking adorable

ASHLEY and *TWILIGHT* costar RACHELLE LEFEVRE work the red carpet.

NIKKI poses with ROSARIO DAWSON.

NIKKI with her costars from *The O.C.* in a 2006 episode

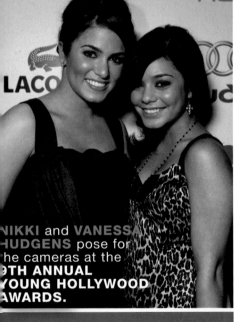
NIKKI and VANESSA HUDGENS pose for he cameras at the 9TH ANNUAL YOUNG HOLLYWOOD AWARDS.

NIKKI
REED

NIKKI shows off her gorgeous smile.

KRISTEN looking glam on the red carpet

A little rain doesn't keep these stars away from the *TWILIGHT* Japan premiere.

KRISTEN STEWART

KRISTEN signs autographs for fans.

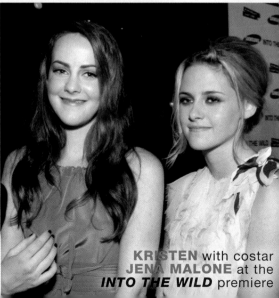

KRISTEN with costar **JENA MALONE** at the *INTO THE WILD* premiere

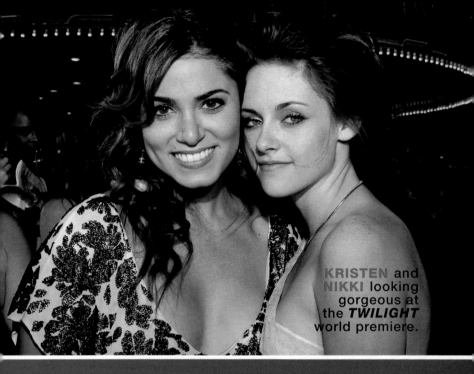

KRISTEN and NIKKI looking gorgeous at the *TWILIGHT* world premiere.

SUPERNATURAL GIRLS

ASHLEY and her *TWILIGHT* costar RACHELLE LEFEVRE show off their long, curly locks.

She admitted to *Vanity Fair*, "When you're playing a character in a book, there's already a lot of pressure because all of the millions of people who have read the series have been able to envision and become very attached to the characters. It wouldn't matter if there was a picture of Rosalie on the cover of the book—everyone would still have their own idea of who she is because everyone relates to the characters in a different way. That, by itself, is very intimidating."

But Nikki held on to her belief that once the fans saw her in character, they would be more accepting. And right she was! The fans thought she did a spectacular job as Rosalie and can't wait to see her reprise the role in the sequels!

Although *Twilight* is the third collaboration between Catherine Hardwicke and Nikki, Nikki is quick to point out that she's not automatically given parts in Catherine's projects just because the two of them are close friends. Nikki also had to get the go-ahead from the rest of the *Twilight* team before Catherine could sign her on. "Unfortunately, what a lot of people don't realize is that when you're making a film, it's not just the director. There are producers; there are a lot of people that make these decisions. And as nice as it would be for Catherine to be able to call me and just say, 'Hey, can I put you in my film?' It doesn't exactly work like that," Nikki told MTV.com.

"Look at [Leonardo] DiCaprio," Nikki continued to alloy.com. "He's worked with the same director for years now. That happens a lot—you find a good team, and [she] and I happen to make a good team."

But if she had a chance to play a different character entirely, Nikki would choose Alice. "There's something about Alice that's just [intriguing]. I'm sure a lot of other people feel this too. Like her psychic abilities . . . and that she was in a mental hospital," Nikki told MTV.com.

Anna Kendrick, like her soon-to-be *Twilight* costars, hadn't read any of the books in Stephenie Meyer's series prior to her audition. "I had no idea what I was getting myself into, to be honest," Anna told MTV.com. "Before I had even read the script, I was telling a friend about it. A couple of his friends, who I didn't really know, overheard. They were big fans of the books! That was one of the first things that got me really excited about it, because they had read them, and they knew all about it. That was the first hint that this was as big as it is."

Considering what happened to poor Anna during her audition, she was probably really glad to have gotten cast! Her audition didn't go quite as she had planned. "It was a straight-up audition situation. They . . . brought me in for a mix-and-match [with various actors]. I was so sick . . . they asked me to stay, and I literally told them I couldn't because I just felt so ill and I had to go home," she told MTV.com.

But the producers called her back, anyway, and eventually Anna was awarded the role of Bella's school friend Jessica Stanley. Anna described her character to MTV.com as "just kind of pathetic. And hopelessly insecure [but] pretends to be confident . . . So it was actually really fun to just be a mess and embarrass myself and make situations as awkward and uncomfortable as possible."

Anna was actually quite well-suited to play Bella's chatterbox friend. The character speaks quite rapidly and excitedly—"[but] it was a cake walk after 'Rocket Science,'" Anna joked to MTV.com.

After she was cast, Anna made up for lost time fast by reading the books back-to-back. "I tore through [the entire series] the second I was cast!" she told MTV.com. Of course every *Twilight* fan can relate to that! And she became more than just an actress playing a role in a movie—she became a true *Twilight* fan. So she must have been very excited to get to play a part in bringing the beloved series to life!

As an up-and-comer on the Hollywood scene, Anna was thrilled with the news that she had won the part of Jessica. Because the character is featured throughout the three other books in the series, Anna knew it was a possibility that she would get additional screen time as the sequels to *Twilight* were developed—and she was right!

Christian Serratos was another up-and-coming Hollywood star looking for her big break. And she definitely found it when the *Twilight* producers contacted her agent about auditioning for a role. Christian was familiar with *Twilight*, so she was very interested in an audition. She had the books on her reading "to do" list, and moved them quickly to the top so she'd be ready for the audition! Like all the other Twilighters out there, Christian devoured the books! She told *Girls' Life*, "I started reading and I could not put the book[s] down for the life of me. I completely lost track of my own life because I was so into [them]. I read them back-to-back and finished *Eclipse* and I was so bummed that I would have to wait so long for *Breaking Dawn*." After reading the books and doing some research about them, Christian realized how big the movie had the potential to be—and admits that knowing that almost made her blow her audition!

"I [had gotten] a call from my agent about this film, and I thought I should probably do my homework and figure out what it was all about," Christian told teenhollywood.com. "And, that's when I saw the slight obsession with it. I was like, 'Oh, don't screw this up,' and I did. I flew all the way from Minden, Nevada, 'cause I was living out there, at the time. I completely messed up the audition, but I guess (director) Catherine Hardwicke knew what she wanted, and she had faith in me and brought me back in. I just flat-out blew the audition. Because I did do my homework, I realized how big it was and I think it psyched me out."

And she went on to explain how the realization of *Twilight*'s blockbuster potential came to her in stages: "I booked [the job] and I was like, 'Wow, this is big!' I filmed it and I was like, 'Well, this is bigger.' And then, I was done and, with the press and the premiere, I was like, 'Wow, this is huge!' I don't think I'll ever be done with, 'Oh, that was big!' I think I'll always just continue to say, 'This is getting bigger.'"

Although Christian eventually won the role of Bella's incredibly sweet and good-natured friend Angela, she actually began the auditioning process by reading for Jessica! At the last minute, the casting directors asked her to read for Angela. Christian was pretty excited about it, because she really liked Angela's character in the books. Christian has worn glasses since she was little, so she decided to wear her own glasses and put her hair in a ponytail during her audition. It was a little detail, but it must have helped, because she eventually won the part—and kept that same look for Angela in the movie!

Christian was totally stoked to be playing Bella's friend Angela. Angela is a bookish, photography-loving student who remains one of Bella's true friends throughout the books. Christian described her character to MTV.com as "very committed to doing her best in school, and [who's] just there to befriend Bella and . . . make sure [Bella] feels comfortable in the new school. She's kind of timid and keeps to herself, but she's very sweet. She's a great girl."

Throughout the film Angela is seen with a camera. On the set, Christian was given an actual working camera to shoot the scenes with. "During scenes I would take lots of pictures, and now I have them all on a memory card. I got some great shots. It was so much fun," she told *Girls' Life*. Hope Christian saved those pictures—they're priceless now!

Casting Angela and Jessica was the final piece of the picture. Now Catherine and the rest of the *Twilight* crew were finally ready to start filming. The girls couldn't wait to bring the characters they loved so much to life on the big screen. And once the cameras were rolling, the *Twilight* girls' lives would never be the same!

CHAPTER 13
Twilight, Cameras, Action!

Twilight was filmed on location in both Portland, Oregon, and Washington State from February to April 2008. Catherine thought it was the perfect place to shoot, because it was close to where the actual books take place, and also because the Pacific Northwest is notorious for gloomy weather—perfect for vampires! But the cast—since they weren't *actual* vampires—didn't love the weather so much. There were days when the weather was more wicked than James, Laurent, and Victoria combined! Its constant changes were a challenge. In one day, the weather could go from sunny to cloudy to raining to hailing to sunny again.

The weather started to weigh on Catherine, too. "There were some days I cried," she admitted to *Entertainment Weekly*. "But then I would see these girls and moms who loved the book standing in the rain [watching], and I'd think, 'I can't have a pity party. I better stand up and make this scene great. I don't care if it is hailing on me.'"

Although Ashley said dealing with the weather was all part of the experience, it could definitely be uncomfortable! "We had to stop shooting a scene because my lips turned purple and I was shaking. I was like, 'I'm from Jacksonville, Florida. I can't deal with the cold!' That was rough," she told *MediaBlvd* magazine.

But Ashley and the rest of the cast knew they had to brave the cold if they wanted to make the movie as authentic as possible. Forks, Washington, the setting for *Twilight*, is supposed to be a very gray and rainy place. Otherwise, the vampires couldn't come outside. "Any other [movie] shoot can't film when there is rain, but we couldn't film if there was sun, so that was difficult," Christian said to *Girls' Life*. "We had to film at night a lot, and those shoots ran for a long time. It was exhausting, but a blast at the same time."

But the girls appreciated being on location for one very important reason: It really helped them become their characters. "When you're on location, it makes it a little easier to transform and become the character, because it is tough [otherwise]. It's a little easier to become the character when you're basically living in a hotel," Ashley told *MediaBlvd* magazine.

When the cast finally arrived on location, they had two weeks to rehearse and learn their lines perfectly before the cameras started rolling. Spending time together in rehearsals not only helped the cast become their characters, it also helped them get to know each other better. In the end, that meant that their chemistry on-screen would be better. But their rehearsals were often a lot more complex than just going over lines together. "We had classes to learn how to behave in the [vampire] roles, like movement [and dance] class," Nikki said to *Vanity Fair*. *Twilight*'s vampires are fast, deadly, but also really graceful. The classes that Ashley and Nikki and the guy vampires took during rehearsals helped them get the feel of actually moving like a vampire. That wasn't the only unique thing about rehearsals. The actors also got trained in wirework and learned how to play baseball for the Cullens' thunderous baseball game up in the mountains!

The girls really loved learning how to fly and jump on wires. Harnesses and cables were used to help the vampires run at super speed and fly through the air with their jumps. Although that sounds like it would be easy—having something pulling you along—it definitely wasn't! The cast found it difficult to maintain their center of gravity, and the cables also hurt because they had a tendency to dig and cause bruises. But overall, the cast found the wirework to be one of the highlights of filming.

Ashley had never done wirework before, and she thought the experience was completely amazing! "I'd never done [anything like] that [before], and now I'm itching to do an action film. Jackson [Rathbone], Kellan [Lutz], and I got to do wirework, where we had to jump off a balcony for the fight sequence with Cam [Gigandet]. That was amazing! It was such a rush! It was so fun! Jumping off the balcony with wires was a free-fall. It was kind of like the Tower of Terror at Disneyland. It was this free-fall, minus the actual encasing. It was so cool! It was so exciting! By the end of the day, we were like, 'I want to do that again!' It was a play day, while at work. We're signed for a second and third film, and I hope there is a ton of wirework in them because it was so amazing," she gushed to *MediaBlvd* magazine.

Although she didn't have to do any wirework to fly since Bella is human, Kristen got to do a bit of her own stunt work in the ballet studio fight scene—and she really got into it! "[I] love doing [stunts]. Many times in the [fight scene], I would do a fall a couple of times or hit my head on the pillars a couple of times, and I wanted to go back and watch [the video playback]. I was like, 'That's [terrible]!' And then, I just literally flung myself into the pillar, and I was like, 'OK, we can't do that again. But we got it!'" she told MTV.com.

The baseball scene is one in particular that required a lot of work from all of the cast in terms of training, special effects, and stunts. Catherine envisioned the game just bursting with energy and action—the characters running incredibly fast and jumping higher than trees, with thunder and lightning crashing in the background. But she knew it wasn't going to be easy to bring her vision to life.

When it came to actually brushing up on their baseball skills, Ashley and Nikki had their work cut out for them. Neither of them had actually ever played baseball before!

For her role, Nikki had to learn how to bat left-handed, so she spent a lot of time at the batting cages. But all that practice didn't make her an expert, just believable as a baseball player in the film. "I would stay far away from me and a bat and a baseball," she joked to MTV.com.

When it came to sliding into the bases and playing some hardcore baseball, Catherine wanted authenticity from her actors. "It's not a joke, working with Catherine," Nikki told the *Los Angeles Times*. "She's not the kind of girl who's like, 'Let's stick you on some pads and bubble wrap and let you slide in a warehouse.' She's like, 'Nikki, there's the field. There's your mud. I'll slap a kneepad on you and a butt-pad and you're going for it.'"

For her part, Ashley had to learn to pitch overhand fastballs because in *Twilight*, Alice is the Cullen family pitcher. Ashley worked with a coach for two weeks to perfect her technique. She found it scary at first because it was a completely new experience—she had never thrown a baseball before in her life! It took her a while to catch on, and there was a time when Catherine wondered if she'd have to use a stunt double for Ashley in the scene. But in typical Ashley fashion, she kept at it and improved enough to be able to film the scene believably. In *Twilight,* Alice pitches about one hundred miles per hour, but Ashley didn't have to worry about being *that* good. The special effects team would take care of making that happen in post-production. But to make the scene work, Ashley still had to accurately throw the baseball right past the camera so the cameraman could get the shot. She actually hit the camera a couple of times—and the poor cameraman at least once! It was a fun experience, but Ashley admits that by the time it was all over, she was pretty sick of baseball!

Acting like a vampire (especially a baseball-playing vampire) took a lot of hard work. But it took just as much work to look like one! The whole cast and crew knew from the very beginning that getting the right look for the vampires was going to be very important to the fans and, ultimately, to the success of the film.

The first step was getting the vampire skin tone right, which proved to be quite a process! The filmmakers didn't want the actors' skin to be freakishly white, like a mime. The vampires in the film are passing as humans, so the makeup artists wanted to find just the right shade of pale, so audiences would really believe in the characters. They experimented with a lot of things, but in the end, the makeup artists used a battery-charged ionizer—which is a lot like a little airbrush—to apply the makeup. The ionizer could get pretty close to the girls' skin, but if it accidentally touched them—ouch! They got a tiny shock of electricity. Talk about the hazards of being beautiful!

To get their vampire-colored eyes, the actresses simply had to wear colored contact lenses—honey-colored for when they weren't hungry, and red for when they needed to feed! While this wasn't nearly as time-consuming of a process as altering the actresses' skin color, it was definitely uncomfortable to have contact lenses constantly being yanked from their eyes!

Of all the *Twilight* actresses, Nikki had to go through the most drastic change to look the part of Rosalie. She had to completely change her hair color, because in the books, Rosalie is a stunning blonde. Initially, Nikki had planned to just wear a blond wig. But at screen tests for *Twilight*, the fans went berserk over this little detail! Some of them were already unhappy about a dark-skinned, dark-haired girl being cast to play the pale, blond Rosalie. A wig wasn't enough to transform Nikki into the character, and it looked fake. Nikki wanted to do whatever she could for the success of the movie, so she made the decision to dye her hair.

It turned out to be quite a job! It took thirty-six hours just to dye the top sections of her hair blond. Plus, every other day, Nikki had to bleach her head and her skin to keep in character. But in the end, it was all worth it. The physical transformation really helped Nikki to feel more like her character. She told alloy.com: "Waking up in the morning and looking at myself looking like that [helped] . . . [For] the sake of not having to spend hours in the makeup chair, I bleached my skin, I exfoliated my skin, I had my hair dyed, my eyebrows dyed, and I was in there every other day, even if I wasn't shooting, making sure my roots weren't showing." Even if the fans didn't support her being cast as Rosalie, Nikki didn't want to let them down. "I really wanted the fans to understand that I was dedicated, and I was going to do whatever I needed to do, even at the expense of going bald," she told MTV.com. Nikki was willing to suffer a little bit for the role, and she did—she actually lost some of her beautiful hair as a result of all the bleaching. "My hair didn't fall out [at] the root[s] . . . [but it] basically broke off to about two inches long," she told alloy.com. Bleaching and dyeing her hair got Nikki through the first movie, but the makeup artists decided to improve this process for the second film by using a wig that doesn't look fake!

Nikki's transformation didn't end there. Like her on-screen sis, Ashley, Nikki had to deal with some height issues. "[I'm] not six feet tall. Ashley Greene is much taller than me in real life, and she plays Alice, who is supposed to be four feet 10 inches. So I was in these monster, hand-crafted heels, like stilts, at all times. You make exceptions when you cast actors, and I had to go the furthest by far. It was fun—a lot of time in the makeup chair!" she said to *Vanity Fair*.

One part of the filming that was more fun than work was rehearsing scenes with the Cullens' fancy cars. Ashley and Jackson especially liked sitting in Dr. Cullen's car. "I think Dr. Cullen's car is [completely cool]. It's a [black Mercedes S55 AMG] . . . and we're like, 'He got the good end of the deal!'" Ashley told MTV.com.

Luckily for the cast, there were a ton of fun moments on the *Twilight* set—with many memories made and friendships formed. All the work they put in, from learning wirework to changing their appearances, was well worth it!

CHAPTER 14

Fun and Friendships on the Set

For *Twilight*'s gorgeous young cast, making the film was incredible for so many reasons. Perhaps first and foremost, it was amazing because the entire cast got along so well, especially the girls. "We had such a big cast, and we were all fairly close in age, and we were together constantly. In that situation you might expect drama to ensue. But we were all so obsessed with this project. We were all focused on the same thing, and it was really creative and ambitious," Kristen said to *Vanity Fair*.

Even though Christian hadn't done a whole lot of film work before *Twilight*, she'd been on enough sets to know bonding when she saw it. "I think [it's] natural, when you're doing a project, especially one like *Twilight* [for the cast to bond]. It's just natural that everyone sticks together. They know what's going on. They know what's up. But, it's been great to work with everyone. We're all around the same age and we all get along. It's a great cast," she explained to iesb.net.

As a relative newcomer to film acting, Ashley had no idea what to expect on the set—and she was pleasantly surprised once filming got underway. Considering all the girls in the cast were relatively inexperienced and under a lot of pressure to bring Stephenie Meyer's wildly popular book series to life, they ended up having a lot of fun together—and making the movie a smash hit! "Everyone was surprisingly really cool. There was no drama. I think we were all so happy to be there, even though everyone has different personalities. I don't think one of us is the same, but we had a blast. We just bonded as a family. The cool part about being able to do the next couple of films is that we do get along so well. It's nice that we're all going to get to work together again. There's no one person we can't stand. There are no love triangles and no drama, or anything like that. We got lucky!" Ashley told *MediaBlvd* magazine.

Christian agreed. "It was really fun to work with

everyone. I felt like I already knew them before going up to film because you hear about everyone. We all knew who was cast before filming, so it was really easy to bond with everyone," she told *Girls' Life.*

There was a lot to laugh about on the set, too. The girls especially loved giggling over Rob's supposed marriage proposals to Kristen! Those rumors caused quite a frenzy in the media and with diehard fans in *Twilight* blogs and other gossip sites. Everybody wanted to know: Were the leading man and his lovely costar actually falling for each other, or was it a publicity stunt meant to get the fans excited (as if they weren't excited enough already!)?

Don't worry, ladies—the rumors aren't true! Rob actually blames himself for that rumor. "I said that in some interview as a joke—'Oh, I proposed to her multiple times.' And then it gets printed: 'On the set, he proposed multiple times,'" he told *GQ.*

And when *GQ* asked Kristen about the rumor, she said that it was just one of Rob's unique personality quirks. "He probably proposes to several girls a day," she said. "It's sort of his thing. He thinks it's cute."

With all the steamy on-screen romance between Bella and Edward, Jasper and Alice, and Rosalie and Emmett, it's no wonder fans are dying to know if there are any real-life romances going on with the hot young cast. "Everybody thinks that because there are so many good-looking cast members, everyone's hanging out and hooking up. It looks like people have blazing chemistry on-screen, so I wouldn't be surprised!" Jackson said to *Seventeen.*

Is this Jackson's way of hinting that there could be something between him and his on-screen wife, Ashley? Not so, according to Ashley. "I have no social life . . . right now it's my career . . . it's very, very difficult to have a boyfriend," she told *Extra TV.* But who knows what the future holds? If only we could ask Alice!

After twelve-hour days of filming, the cast would often go to dinner together. Portland has some wonderful restaurants, so they always looked forward to trying new places. "We did a lot of group dinners with the whole cast," Nikki told alloy.com. "Like, we would go to this one restaurant called Jake's every couple of nights. We'd all go, and the poor manager finally got so sick of [us] going like, 'Hi, reservation for 26!' It was tons of fun, no matter what."

If they didn't go out to dinner, the whole gang would order room service instead and sit around in their hotel rooms, talking or watching movies. There were lots of nights where some of the cast would play guitar and sing. Or they'd go to a neighborhood karaoke joint and actually take the stage. Bet the fans who happened to be there at the time loved that!

In fact, love of music was a common bond among the young cast. "Every member of the cast was musically inclined or interested," Kristen said to *Teen Vogue*. Kristen herself plays the guitar, Rob Pattinson plays the guitar and piano, and Jackson Rathbone is actually in a band called 100 Monkeys. Jackson told *Seventeen* magazine, "Rob [Pattinson] and I both played a lot of music. I'm in a band, and Rob's also a musician, a singer-songwriter. We went to an open-mike night a couple times that was right next door to the hotel. The first time, we just got up onstage and jammed with Nikki and Kristen. It was fun!" He went on to praise his lovely costars for their musical chops. "Nikki and I started writing songs together, and Kristen is actually a pretty sick guitar player."

When not doing impromptu jam sessions with one another, watching other bands play was a big part of how the cast spent time off the set. "Nikki got me into Laura Marling, [who] is rad . . . [We saw] her at Hotel Café," Anna told MTV.com. "I also went to see [Rob Pattinson play a show] one night. I remembered seeing that he played guitar . . . and then I heard him sing, and I was like, 'This is just not fair!' He has an awesome voice, and it was like, 'This is an uneven distribution of wealth!'"

All that bonding off the set really helped Kristen and Nikki in particular become very close friends. They certainly had a lot in common! They were close in age, they both started working in movies when they were very young, and they often played similar characters—troubled teenage girls. Nikki told *Vanity Fair*, "Kristen Stewart and I became really close . . . It's very common to become close with [a cast when on location], and then everyone goes back to their lives. It's very hard on the heart. I think that as a person you become very callous. You become very aware that things are transient—they come, they go.

Kristen and I had a very natural progression to our friendship. She was in rehearsal on her own a lot, as was I, but we became very close over the months and now I'm like a part of her family." And Kristen felt the same way, telling the magazine, "Nikki Reed and I became really, really good friends. She's really smart and funny." Plus, it helped that neither Kristen nor Nikki were into the party scene—even though Nikki often gets labeled as a "party girl" because of characters she's played in movies! Instead, the two girls tended to pass the time reading and writing and hanging out at each other's trailers or hotel rooms. They walked around, went to street fairs, talked all night, and watched movies together. Exactly the same kind of stuff that every girl does with her best friend!

Even if Rosalie and Bella weren't exactly the best of friends, Kristen and Nikki were! The girls actually thought it was hysterical that on-screen, they were enemies. "It's going to be really fun when we [film *New Moon*] and I'm doing the scenes with Kristen where I hate her," Nikki told about.com.

Rosalie doesn't love Bella, but one vampire who

does is Alice! Given that Alice loves Bella like a sister, it certainly helped that Ashley and Kristen also got along very well. "I think Kristen and I are lucky in that we have extremely different personalities but we get along. She's the youngest, except for Taylor [Lautner, who plays Jacob Black], but she has a lot more under her belt. And she's very mature and down to earth. So it was really nice working with her," Ashley told film.com.

Kristen was an all-around well liked person on the set. On top of everything else, she got to be good friends with her costar and on-screen love interest, Rob Pattinson. "He's like a little tortured artist. He's British. He's tall. He always looks like he's thinking about something. And he's quite witty," she said to *People*. Rob is equally complimentary of Kristen. When asked by MTV to list the top five reasons it was great to be Edward Cullen, he could only name one: He got to kiss Kristen Stewart!

Of course filming a movie like *Twilight*—with a big cast, and lots of crazy stunts and special effects and unpredictable weather—would result in lots of memorable and favorite moments for the cast.

One of those memories for Christian Serratos was the beach scene where the Forks High School students mingle with the La Push kids. She told *Popstar*, ". . . Justin [Chon, who plays Eric] had to chase me, and he was covered in seaweed and algae. It was disgusting, and it was touching me, and it was gross, and it was making all the sand stick to me. But it was so much fun . . . !"

But her absolute favorite scene to shoot was the one where Angela, Bella, and Jessica try on dresses for the prom. "[T]hey were just funky, out-there dresses," Christian added. "Plus I like that we were inside instead of out in the cold." Considering how bad the weather was, it's no surprise that Christian picked this as her favorite scene!

One of Anna's most memorable moments involved Taylor Lautner, who plays Jacob Black. Taylor is an experienced martial artist, and one day he was talking about his ability to do a standing backflip, which is a really difficult move to master. So Justin Chon dared him to do it! But Anna was worried that Taylor would break his neck, so she tried to convince him not to. At the time, Taylor was wearing heavy boots—not exactly the best gear for a dangerous martial arts move! But after about ten minutes of being egged on, Taylor suddenly busted out an awesome backflip. "That was kind of crazy," Anna told MTV.com.

No surprise here—Jessica and Angela's scene with Edward was one of Anna's favorite scenes to shoot. The script called for Jessica and Angela to be "dazzled" by Edward. It was probably really easy for Anna to get all googly-eyed at Edward because Rob is so cute! But Anna had a little more trouble with the whole "being dazzled by him" part of the scene. In fact, Anna struggled not to laugh the whole time, because Rob kept looking at her with what was supposed to be his "charming" smile, but wound up looking like he was trying hard not to laugh. And that made *her* laugh! "But it actually ended up working because essentially it was uncomfortable laughter, and it made sense that I would be fighting these almost, like, church giggles," Anna explained to MTV.com.

The cast also had fun debating what life would actually be like as a vampire—and who on the cast would make a good one! Christian told MTV.com that she would probably choose to become a vampire if she could—out of pure curiosity! She blames that same curiosity on the power she'd pick if she were lucky enough to have a vampire talent—Edward's power of reading people's minds. "I am a very curious person that has to know everything," she told popstar.com.

As far as who would make a good vampire in real life, Kristen thinks Nikki would, because she always seems to get what she wants. And Nikki thinks Kristen is already sort of like a vampire because she prefers the night, while Nikki prefers the day.

Of course, being a vampire isn't all fun and games—it also requires living forever. The thought of that wasn't appealing to either Nikki or Kristen. Kristen claimed she'd simply go crazy with all that time on her hands! And Nikki told alloy.com, "I want drive. I want something to motivate me. I feel like time being a factor in the equation of life makes you feel the pressure to accomplish things. I know that by the time I'm 23, I want to direct a full-length feature and I have like milestones that I want to hit and I think that that comes from time being a part of that. If I could live forever I feel like I'd never want to accomplish anything. There's pressure with time."

But Nikki and Kristen agreed that, if they had to choose one member of the cast to spend eternity with, it would be each other. Talk about true friendship! "We jive. I can handle her for longer periods than five minutes," Kristen told alloy.com.

And that's definitely a good thing—especially since there are more *Twilight* movies to make!

CHAPTER 15

A Total Fan-omenon

Take one epic "first love" story between a beautiful teenage girl who's a bit of loner and a smokin' hot vampire who's been seventeen for nearly one hundred years. Then mix that with millions of passionate—call them bloodthirsty!—fans. Voilà! You've got the magic formula for a blockbuster film, a number one selling DVD, and a cast of relatively unknown actors being catapulted overnight into Hollywood's hottest stars.

Despite their varying levels of experience with film and TV, none of the actors from *Twilight* were prepared for what was to come in terms of fan reaction. After all, how do you prepare for something that's truly once-in-a-lifetime?

"I knew that we had a devoted fan base, but I thought it was exclusive. I thought [*Twilight*] was going to be a cult movie. Well, I was wrong," Kristen admitted to blackbookmag.com.

"You don't really know what to do," Ashley said to *Vanity Fair*. "That's the thing. I hadn't really done anything major and then this came about, so it's kind of surreal. It's been amazing so far and, speaking for myself, and I think for everybody else, the fans are really supportive and it's all been really good. I'm enjoying it right now and it's really exciting, as long as people don't, you know, follow me home. I think that Robert Pattinson might have that problem, but I think that I'm in the clear."

Much of the credit for the buzz build-up goes to Summit Entertainment, the movie company that brought *Twilight* to the silver screen. The studio was very smart about the way it marketed the movie to the books' large, devoted, Web-savvy fan base.

Weeks before the movie came out, Summit put together the *Twilight* Tour—a mall tour involving meet-and-greets and question-and-answer sessions with several of the films' stars. In some cases, there were near riots as thousands of fans turned out for these events. Fans who stood in line to get an autograph and thirty seconds of face time with their favorite stars were tearful and tongue-tied. At the Q&A sessions with the stars, it was typical for there to be so much screaming that the audience couldn't even hear the actors' responses! But it was all good for the fans—because they were perfectly happy just looking at their beloved characters.

But Kristen totally understands why fans reacted this way. "[*Twilight*] is a very passionate book, so it makes sense that the audience would be as hardcore," she said in an interview with *Access Hollywood* before *Twilight*'s theatrical release. "They're already going crazy over the hot vampires." But in some cases, it wasn't all fun and games, and the chaos was downright scary for the actors. At one event at a mall in San Francisco, thousands more fans showed up to see Rob Pattinson than were expected—with only one security guard on duty to try to control the crowd! It was dangerous, so the event had to be canceled. The fans were disappointed, of course, but it only made them clamor to meet their favorite blood-sucking stars even more!

As the movie's main star, things were tough for

Rob, but it wasn't any easier for the *Twilight* girls to deal with passionate fans. Kristen told the *Los Angeles Times* blog, "In Rome, I was literally thrown into a van. I was being held by my arms by two big security guys, and they were getting pushed over by these 15-year-old girls, and they let me go for like a second, and I just got enveloped. The bodyguards had to pick me up and shove me into the van. But then the van starts rocking because the barricades had broken down and they swarmed the car. It was totally scary." Kristen's good friend Nikki worried about all the attention Kristen was getting. Nikki told the *USA Weekend* blog, "It's really overwhelming for everybody, especially for [Kristen] and Rob and Taylor Lautner. Actually, any of the boys and Kristen. It's really overwhelming to hear the screams of these girls."

Even though the attention was positive because it meant that fans were really excited about the film, it was also really exhausting. "It's not normal for me to be in a situation that *Twilight* puts you in," Kristen explained to E! Online. "It's not personally normal for me to see 5,000 screaming girls." Kristen admits dealing with all the fan hysteria isn't always easy for her. But she understands that for the most part, the rabid fans love Bella, not her personally. "They're not screaming for me, I could be anybody and it's really bizarre to find yourself in the position of figurehead for so many people who are obsessed with your character," she said to the *USA Weekend* blog. "And it's so weird, too, because it's such a personal thing for me: I'm obsessed with my character, too, and I care about the book just as much as they do."

But Kristen also really loves her fans! And she loves that she has had the opportunity to bring Bella's character to life for them. "Everyone's so awesome and positive and great. Usually I do movies that don't see the light of day, so this is the über-opposite . . . and you work so hard on something and you're so proud and this is what you do it for. It's pretty great!" she gushed to ET Online.

And, she continued, the enthusiasm and energy of the fans definitely pushes you to do your best work. "You have to give yourself a couple pep talks every once in a while. But it's a good motivator."

Since Kristen plays *Twilight's* main female character, it's not surprising that she gets tons of attention, but what about the rest of the girls? The fans love them, too! Christian plays a relatively minor role in the film, but even she admits that she gets recognized on the street frequently, something she's definitely not used to! Fans recognize Christian easily, because she wore her own glasses in the movie, so she actually looks a lot like herself on-screen. Be on the lookout, *Twilight* fans—if you see a girl who looks a lot like Christian, it's probably her!

Getting recognized is a really new—but cool—experience for Christian. "When I booked *Twilight* and people started calling me Christian instead of a character name, I was like, '[Wow]!' That was so weird to me. After doing [*Ned's Declassified*], everyone called me by my character's name and I was like, 'That's cool. They recognized me.' But, when they start calling you by your real name, that's when you know it's big. I remember I went to the bank and the teller girls at the window started freaking out and had me sign *Breaking Dawn* books. I was like, 'This is weird!'" she told teenhollywood.com.

Twilight fans are loyal, and have many awesome ways of showing their favorite actors and actresses their love! For example, one creative (and totally hooked up!) fan actually sent the names of a bunch of people involved in the *Twilight* movie—the actors, Catherine Hardwicke, Stephenie Meyer, screenwriter Melissa Rosenberg, and others—into space as part of NASA's Kepler Mission! According to the official NASA certificate of participation that everyone received, the Kepler Mission is "NASA's first mission capable of finding Earth-size planets orbiting other stars in our galaxy." How cool is that? The *Twilight* stars actually got the chance to have their names floating in space next to *real* stars!

Overall, the actors have found the passion of the fans to be one of the most motivating, energizing parts of their whole *Twilight* experience. On the red carpet at the L.A. premiere of *Twilight,* Anna was asked what she thought of the fans, many of whom had been lined up since the previous night for the opportunity to get a glimpse of their favorite stars. "I think they're unbelievable. I knew it was going to be intense and I knew it was going to be loud . . .

[but] they're so supportive and warm and amazing," she told about.com.

Ashley also felt her costar's excitement and shared her appreciation of the crowd. "It's quite amazing. It's a really great feeling to walk in there and have people chanting your name and be just as passionate about a film as I am."

So why all the fan-demoneum? What is it about *Twilight*—both the book and the movie—that makes it so popular? Christian has her own theory: "Especially [for] the female audience, [because] it's the first love . . . [and] it's told from Bella's point of view. Every girl sees [herself] as Bella . . . which I totally did!" she said to about.com. Ashley offers a similar perspective: "[For] the guys it's a different kind of vampire story and it does have the sports and the fight scenes and all those elements. But when it boils down to it, it's a really kind of epic love story. It's the story about two people who just can't bear to be away from each other and I think everybody wants that, and everybody relates to that. And then you throw in the superhero powers and the glory of being a vampire and it just hits on every level."

And Ashley can certainly identify with the fans when it comes to the character of Edward. ". . . [I] was in love with Edward, too. I'm not going to lie. I was like, 'Where is this guy? Where does he exist? Where can I find him?' So I was just as in love with the story as everybody else, and then I got to film it. It's been amazing," she told about.com.

Stephenie Meyer wanted to make sure that the movie turned out perfectly for all the fans who were anxiously awaiting its release. Even though she didn't write the script, she did play a major part in making sure the script stayed true to her book—and that included changing things around, when need be. "You know the line 'So the lion fell in love with the lamb'? It's a bit of a cheesy line, I have to say. [The filmmakers] had changed the wording on that, to downplay it a little. And I said, 'I really like how you've changed this, but this line is tattooed on people's ankles. I think you're going to have a problem if you don't do it exactly right.' And they listened to me—and saved themselves the outrage of the people who know these books," Stephenie told *Entertainment Weekly*.

Summit's brilliant marketing tactics worked perfectly, and on its opening weekend, *Twilight* debuted at the number 1 spot at the box office and brought in nearly $70 million. It's gone on to earn over $380 million worldwide.

In its continued efforts to communicate with the *Twilight* fan base, two days after the movie opened, Kristen and Rob, on behalf of Summit, sent a special e-mail to fans confirming the studio's decision to move ahead with *New Moon*. According to ET Online, the email from Kristen and Rob stated:

"We just heard from Summit that we'll be moving forward on *New Moon*. We look forward to sharing this next chapter with you! From every city, every stop, every interview we have done, you've made this an unbelievable, nearly surreal experience . . . and so cool that we were all in this together."

As the DVD release drew nearer, Summit once again used in-store events to bring out the fans. On the eve of the DVD's release, members of the cast were sent around the country to midnight DVD release parties at retailers. Dubbed "*Twilight* at Midnight," Ashley and Nikki were among the cast sent to locations in major cities like Los Angeles, New York, Chicago, and Dallas.

"It became really important to make the DVD an event," Nancy Kirkpatrick, president of worldwide marketing at Summit Entertainment, told the *Wall Street Journal.*

And an event it was! Over two thousand fans showed up at a Hot Topic in Los Angeles for Ashley Greene's appearance. Ashley was completely blown away by the fan support, and told *People* magazine, "It's every actor's dream, I think, to be part of something that's going to be remembered in history as part of this huge phenomenon."

Summit's strategy for the DVD paid off big time. More than three million DVDs were sold the first day which, according to a press release issued by the studio, made *Twilight* one of the top five best first day DVD releases over the past two years. This put the little-film-that-could in the company of big budget, Hollywood blockbusters like *Pirates of the Caribbean: At World's End, The Dark Knight, Harry Potter and the Order of the Phoenix,* and *Transformers.*

Amazingly, the fan hysteria still didn't die down after the DVD release. When the 2009 MTV Movie Awards were announced, *Twilight* was nominated in six categories and won for five—including Best Kiss, Best Picture, and Kristen herself won for Best Female Performance. When accepting the MTV Movie Awards' signature golden popcorn trophy—which was presented to them by gorgeous actress Sandra Bullock and hunky Ryan Reynolds—Kristen Stewart and Rob Pattinson really gave the fans something to scream about. The two actors came *this close* to reenacting their sultry kiss from the movie!

After Rob fiddled with something up at the podium—"I need to remove my gum," he explained (which naturally prompted enthusiastic screaming and catcalls!), he turned and faced Kristen. She looked up at him, hands on hips, but kept a small distance between them. Rob continued to fidget up onstage, tugging at his shirt, pulling his blazer, rubbing his face, and pushing back that glorious hair! Then he got very still, closed his eyes, puckered up, and waited.

Kristen, alternately looking up at him and gazing down at the ground, began inching toward him. As she got closer, she crossed her arms in a protective gesture . . . but continued her slow dance into him, glancing up at him almost warily. In pure Edward fashion, Rob's facial expression looked like he was literally drinking in her scent!

Then, when their foreheads were barely touching, Kristen's eyes slipped shut—and Rob's lips bent down toward her—and all of a sudden, Kristen drew her face away from his, turned into the microphone with an expression of delighted surprise on her face, and said enthusiastically to the crowd, "Thank you *so* much!" And she picked up the trophy, leaving poor Rob standing there with his mouth hanging open! The audience went wild— they definitely wouldn't have minded at all if the twosome had seen that kiss all the way through!

When Kristen accepted her award for Best Female Performance, she made sure to acknowledge those who made the movie the phenomenon it was—the fans, or as she called them in her shout-out, "the ultimate driving force"!

And that they are—so much so that MTV returned the love in a very cool way: by naming the *Twilight* fan base—which really *had* made all the hype and history possible—its 2008 Woman of the Year!

CHAPTER 16
Shining Stars, *New Moon*

Thanks to the passion and support of Twilighters everywhere—who, in some cases, saw the movie in theaters multiple times!—*Twilight* shattered expectations at the box office. That prompted Summit Entertainment to quickly green-light the next two installments in the series, *New Moon* and *Eclipse*. *Twilight's* success also transformed the actresses overnight into in-demand stars. From film offers to awards to inclusions in "most beautiful" lists, the girls were besieged with it all.

When an actor is suddenly catapulted into the spotlight after appearing in a Hollywood blockbuster, the movie roles tend to come pouring in! And what was Kristen's reaction to this exciting development?

"I told my agent, 'I'm not doing a big movie after *Twilight*,'" she said to film.com. Instead, Kristen went right back to her favorite genre, signing on for a role in *Welcome to the Rileys*, a film starring James Gandolfini and Oscar nominee Melissa Leo. The pair play a married couple grieving the loss of their teenage daughter. Kristen plays a sixteen-year-old dancer who meets Gandolfini's character at a club and unwittingly helps the couple recover from their heartbreak. The movie does not yet have a release date.

In an upcoming part that's already causing lots of buzz—most notably because she chopped off a lot of her hair to rock a black, shaggy 'do—Kristen has been tapped to play rocker Joan Jett in *The Runaways,* a film chronicling the rise and fall of her hard rocking all-girl band of the same name. In the 1970s, the girls in the band were all teenagers, but that didn't stop them from achieving huge success. The Runaways were important in rock history because they achieved legitimate musical success with hit songs, platinum records, and tours, all at an incredibly young age, and during a time when female rock stars weren't quite as commonplace.

But what's most exciting about this film for Kristen Stewart fans everywhere: She has hinted that she will do her own singing in the film! The young actress is definitely qualified. After all, she did a great job strumming her guitar and singing in *Into the Wild*. On top of that, *Twilight* fans will be thrilled to know that Kristen's *New Moon* costar, Dakota Fanning, will play Cherie Currie, the lead singer of the band.

This was Kristen's first time playing a character based on a real person in a movie, and she really looked forward to the challenge. She even spent New Year's Eve 2009 with Joan Jett herself to get to know her and her life story better. It was an amazing, once-in-a-lifetime experience. "She's so cool, one of the nicest, most soulful women I've ever met. And so many people love and admire her. It's an immense responsibility to play a real person, one of the most intimidating things that I've ever had to confront [as an actress]," Kristen told *Parade*. "Her story is an incredibly triumphant, feminist story. The main thing that Joan talked about was just how much she cared about the days when she was a teenager and started singing with The Runaways. She told me that the band was what started her entire life."

Luckily, Kristen's success in *Twilight* meant she was able to be pickier about choosing roles. And for her, that meant going back to her roots and acting in a lot more indie films. "[The success of *Twilight*] has been good for me," she told *The Insider*. "It really facilitates work that I love. It makes it much easier. I don't have to fight to get into a movie that I really want to do . . . and it was [before]." Plus, Kristen's rising star means that more attention will be given to the movies that she acts in, which is especially beneficial for independent films, which tend to not get as much publicity as movies with a big budget and wide release. Kristen has always loved indies, so she really treasures being able to help the movies she loves in any way she can. "[That] part is good," she told the *San Francisco Chronicle*. "I want as many people as possible to see [these] movie[s]."

But there's one movie that Kristen is probably *really* looking forward to working on. It's called *K-11*, and Kristen is starring in it with her close friend Nikki, *and* her mother, Jules, cowrote it and is directing! It doesn't get much better than that!

This movie is going to be a totally new

experience for both Kristen and Nikki, because they actually both play guys! The film's name—*K-11*—refers to a little known section of the Los Angeles county jail where inmates are kept if they are at risk of being harmed or harassed by the general prison population—for example, if they are celebrities or have committed certain crimes. Kristen is playing a boy named Butterfly while Nikki is playing a man called Mousey. "I thought it was difficult stepping into Rosalie's shoes! It's gonna be a lot more difficult stepping into Mousey's shoes," Nikki joked to MTV.com. The duo hopes to squeeze in this project between filming *New Moon* and *Eclipse*.

For her part, after *Twilight* Nikki also added executive producer to her résumé for an independent film called *The Last Days of Summer* (she also stars in the film!). Nikki plays the character of Stefanie alongside her good friend DJ Qualls, with whom she appeared in *Familiar Strangers*. DJ plays a schizophrenic named Joe who kidnaps Stefanie, and the two spend a day together.

Besides acting, Nikki is working on writing more screenplays and has set her sights on directing in the future. "So if you asked me if I wanted to be an actor forever, the answer would be no. It never has been and it never will be something that I want to spend the rest of my life doing. I respect that [is] what Kristen wants to do forever . . . It's just there's another angle that I would like to approach film [from]," she explained to about.com.

As far as Ashley's career, appearing in *Twilight* was just the launching pad that she had been dreaming about since arriving in L.A. as a seventeen-year-old. But the buzz about the pretty actress actually started before the movie even came out! "Usually, as an actor, you get the attention after you've released a couple big films. It's interesting to have that before," she told *MediaBlvd* magazine.

Ashley is especially grateful that fame hit when it did, and not when she was a few years younger. Her maturity and experience meant that she was better able to handle her newfound fame. "If everything that's happening to me now, happened a couple years ago, I wouldn't have known what to do with it because I was so young. I'm this little girl from Jacksonville, Florida. It's been an interesting journey, but I'm really happy with the way everything's worked out," she told *MediaBlvd* magazine.

Thanks to *Twilight*, Ashley has become a household name—although her adoring family is doing their part to keep her grounded! Ashley good-naturedly told her hometown news station, First Coast News, that her newfound success hadn't upped her status at home at all. "My family could [not] care less," she said. "They're still, like, 'You're gonna wash the dishes!'"

With her family's support, Ashley was determined to be extra careful about choosing the right roles. Part of that was finding somebody to model her career after. If Ashley had to pick an actress whose career she admires, it's Charlize Theron. She thinks Charlize chooses inspiring roles, plays strong female characters, and moves people with her performances. "I want to stay away from the typical high school characters, like the hot girl and the mean girl. That's boring. You don't get to transform. I don't want to stick to one genre or one role. I definitely want to do an action film and be a superhero, I want to play a villain, I want to do a period piece, and I want to do a love story. I want to do a little bit of everything. The hard-edged characters are a little more difficult for me to pull off because I have an innocent-looking face. But, hair and makeup, and coaching and attitude always help," she told *MediaBlvd* magazine about her own acting aspirations.

With that in mind, Ashley accepted several other film offers between wrapping *Twilight* and starting *New Moon*. She won her first leading role in the horror movie *Summer's Blood*. In this film, slated for release in 2009, Ashley plays the character of Summer, a hard-edged, troubled girl who leaves her drug-addicted mother to search for her father. While trying to find him, she gets kidnapped. Despite the heavy material, it was a really great and challenging role that Ashley knew she couldn't turn down. "You see this hard character slowly start to break down and go through a lot of stuff, mentally as well as physically. And then, she becomes determined to try to get away. It was really fun. It was a good character to play. It was a little difficult, at times, because it's hard to be in that dark of a place, but I think it's going to be good. I'm really proud of it," Ashley told *MediaBlvd* magazine.

After that, Ashley scored another leading role in the independent movie *Skateland*. Set in Louisiana in 1983, it's a coming-of-age story about the troubles that teens deal with growing up. It was an especially fun movie to film because it was set in the 1980s—so when she was in costume and sporting her big '80s hair, Ashley actually looked a lot like her mom when she was younger! *Skateland* is tentatively scheduled to be released later in 2009 or sometime in 2010.

Ashley also reunited with her hunky *Twilight* costar Kellan Lutz, who plays Emmett Cullen, for an upcoming movie called *Warrior*. In this drama, Ashley plays Brooklyn (a.k.a. Brooke), and Kellan plays Conor Sullivan, a lacrosse player who turns rebellious after his marine corps father dies in combat. His mom sends him to a tough lacrosse training camp led by his father's old friend. Brooke is the coach's daughter—and Conor's love interest! How crazy is it that Ashley and Kellan go from brother and sister in *Twilight* to boyfriend and girlfriend in *Warrior*? Considering the two are long-time friends, the film will probably be a blast to make together. Its expected release date is late 2009 or early 2010.

Ashley also decided to use her newfound celebrity to help a good cause. In early 2009, she became the celebrity spokesperson for donatemydress.org, an organization which encourages girls to donate their prom and other special occasion dresses to others who need them through local "dress drives" across the country. Ashley even has her own special advice when it comes to getting ready for prom or another fancy, formal gathering—in her case, red carpet appearances! "If you wear Jimmy Choo [shoes], in particular, they're not comfortable at all, but they look really, really good. So if you go to Rite Aid or Walgreens, and you get this Band-Aid blister block that you put on before you put on your shoes. It saves your life, every time!" she told *Seventeen*. Considering how much of a fashionista Alice Cullen is—and the fact that she helped Bella get ready for her own prom—this is the perfect cause for Ashley to be involved in!

Even though Anna's role in *Twilight* as Bella's friend Jessica Stanley was a relatively small part, it resulted in big opportunities for the actress! In fact, her scene-stealing turn as Jessica landed her on *Entertainment Weekly*'s list: "Rising Stars: Nine to Watch in 2009."

Anna got right to work on other projects after *Twilight* wrapped. First she signed on for a supporting role in the screen adaptation of the graphic novel *Scott Pilgrim vs. the World*. The movie is about a twenty-three-year-old guy, played by the comedic genius Michael Cera from *Juno*, who falls for the new girl in town and must defeat the girl's seven evil ex-boyfriends in order to win her heart. Anna plays the role of Stacey Pilgrim, the title character's sister. The movie is scheduled for release in 2010.

And on the day *Twilight* landed in theaters, it was announced that Anna had beaten out a bunch of other young actresses, reportedly including *Juno* star Ellen Page and *The Devil Wears Prada* actress Emily Blunt, for the female lead opposite George Clooney in the movie *Up in the Air*, directed by Jason Reitman, who also directed 2007's runaway hit *Juno*.

In the movie, Clooney plays a hardened "career transition counselor" (a guy who fires people for a living!) who loves collecting frequent flyer miles. Anna's character Natalie is a rising star employee who threatens to derail his goal of obtaining his millionth mile.

Like Anna, Christian also benefited a ton from her role as Angela in *Twilight*. In fact, she nabbed a Young Artist Award for Best Performance in a Feature Film—Supporting Young Actress for her work on the film! She was also named one of *People* magazine's "100 Most Beautiful People of 2009." And she shot a video message for PETA—which stands for People for the Ethical Treatment of Animals—to help prevent the slaughter of seals. Some *Twilight* fans might not know that Christian is a vegetarian, and she loves animals and doesn't want to see them hurt. In fact, she wrote on her official MySpace page that she asked for her character Angela to be dressed in clothing that did not use any animal products—and the studio did that for Christian!

Christian will also be launching jewelry and clothing lines in the near future. This isn't a new interest—she's actually been making clothes for years. "I started just taking in clothes that I bought from the store, and I was like, 'Why am I paying money for something that I'm just going to edit anyway?', so I just started making my own stuff, just to go out on a daily basis. And then, I started getting compliments on it, from people wanting to literally buy the clothes off my back," she told teenhollywood.com. "I thought that [starting a clothing line] would definitely be something that would be fun to do. And, plus, my mom's a jewelry designer and I've always made jewelry. I was selling to stores when I was eight years old."

Like her fellow cast members, Christian is excited to see what other opportunities are in store for her. "I've gotten word of a lot of cool projects, but there have been scheduling conflicts. But, I think *Twilight* has brought me crazier stuff [to pursue], which I love," she confessed to teenhollywood.com.

Of course, while all of the film offers and other accolades were completely amazing and totally appreciated by the girls, at the end of the day they were really looking forward to getting back together to start filming *New Moon*. And with all the activity surrounding *Twilight*'s theatrical release, the press tours, and the subsequent DVD release, the cast's reunion came quickly! Filming for *New Moon* took place from late March 2009 through late May 2009 in locations throughout Vancouver, British Columbia, Canada, and Italy—where the Volturi reside! With a new director, more intricate special effects (including Bella's cliff dive!), the introduction of the werewolves, and Edward's departure (at least for a little while), filming *New Moon* promised to be more of a blast than *Twilight*—if that was even possible!

Filming *New Moon* was particularly special for Kristen because she got to celebrate her nineteenth birthday on April 9 with her castmates. According to *People*, everyone on the set serenaded her with "Happy Birthday," and a cake was served during the lunch break. Kristen kept the celebration going that night with a party at a trendy restaurant called Chill Winston—and again the next night, when the gang enjoyed a steak and seafood dinner at Rodney's Oyster House.

Kristen's birthday was a total blast, but there were a ton of other highlights on the set, too. Adorable Ashley was ecstatic to film her favorite moment from the book—where Alice steals a yellow

Porsche in Italy! "It was really fun. I worked with a stuntman before actually driving it and learned how to do a bunch of unnecessary things that were fun, like fishtailing, and he was gonna teach me drifting," Ashley gushed to MTV.com. "I drove it in a scene and came about two inches from the wall!"

Wow—first a fabulous wardrobe for fashionista Alice, then a yellow Porsche! How great is it to be Ashley?

And Christian was just as stoked to be back on the set as Angela. But she knew right away that things were going to be much different this time around. Her first clue? An umbrella!

As soon as she arrived for her first day of work, an assistant director hurried up to her with an umbrella. During modeling shoots, when it's really hot, umbrellas are put over the models, so Christian thought that was what the crew member was doing.

"I was like, 'Oh no, you don't have to do that. It's not that bad out.' And, [the assistant director] was like, 'No, it's for the paparazzi,' and I was like, 'Oh, my God, is that really how it's going to be this time? Seriously?' Every time any one of the cast

189

members went anywhere, they had to have guys with umbrellas around them because there were that many paparazzi. Just going outside and seeing dozens of people with signs, as if it's a concert. It was weird," Christian told teenhollywood.com.

In fact, according to the television news show *Entertainment Tonight*, the movie set was so top secret that there were back alley entrances, fake names on call sheets, and mounted police guarding the set. If anything, the *Twilight* phenomenon was just getting bigger! You'll just have to check out *New Moon* to see how it all came together in the end!

CHAPTER 17

Vampire Glamour: Sparkling On (and Off) the Red Carpet

Kristen Stewart's fashion style is a lot like her movie role choices—she wears what she likes and what she's comfortable in and doesn't much care who's watching or what they might think. It's just one more aspect of her independent spirit that sets her apart from other actresses her age.

In fact, Kristen considers herself a very typical girl. "I look like everyone," she told *Vanity Fair* when asked to describe her trademark style—although she harbors a fondness for things that are beat-up. "I kind of like to look like a hobo," she confessed to the magazine.

Catherine Hardwicke, the director of *Twilight*, told MTV.com, "Kristen's very cas[ual]. She's got her cool, skinny jeans and her rock star T-shirt and she's very chill and down to earth."

When it comes to being viewed as a "style icon,"

the born-and-bred Valley girl is baffled. Kristen really can't understand all the fuss that's made about actors' appearances—and, more importantly, why the way they look should affect their success.

"It's such a bizarre thing, to me, to consider that what I wear, what I do with my hair, affects my career," she told *Teen Vogue*. "I'm not the type of person who has a million things in my closet to put together, so I've begun to work with a stylist and we've started to figure out what I like. Simple, classically pretty things; I love Chanel."

The best way to describe Kristen's look—whether on or off the red carpet—is rocker chic with a touch of goth glamour. Skinny jeans, rock T-shirts, and tank tops are definitely her favorites. She may wear the T-shirts in a variety of ways—cropped, knotted at the waist, or paired with a buttoned cardigan—but the color palette is generally limited to black, gray, or white. Every once in a while, though, Kristen will pop up wearing something fun and colorful as a contrast—like a bright yellow hoodie or a pair of bright red pumps.

Levi's are one of her favorite brands of jeans

because they're comfy and hang just right. Her favorites are her vintage 501s. And she definitely gets the rocker chick vibe going when she wears her black leather bomber jacket—either with skinny jeans or with the minidresses she prefers to wear for her many events, appearances, and photo shoots.

Unless she's rocking the red carpet in a pair of black spiky T-straps or Christian Louboutin pumps, Kristen is likely to be found running around in her sneakers. She admits to having an obsession with sneakers—the older, the better. "I go on eBay all the time to find . . . old sneakers from the '90s that I saw my older brothers wearing," she told *Nylon*.

And she definitely covets her Converse—she wears them with everything! At the 2009 MTV Movie Awards in Universal City, California, she added a funky touch to an otherwise high-fashion look to create an edgy style that's become classic Kristen. By pairing a belted black and red minidress with black Converse sneakers, and wearing her long brown hair swinging loose with dark eye makeup, she looked every bit the picture of vampire chic.

And on the flip side, for a casual event, she'll

wear her Converse with a pair of black cropped pants, a white graphic tee, and a preppy red-striped blazer.

But make no mistake about this California-cool chick. She definitely turns heads when she turns on the glamour! At the Hollywood premiere of *Twilight* at the Mann Theatre Village, Kristen looked every bit the vampire love interest in a Balenciaga red, white, and silver one-shouldered minidress with black pumps. She kept the accessories simple, wearing only a slim silver necklace—which matched the midsection of her dress—and carrying a black clutch. Her hair was vamped up in an updo that showed off silver eye makeup and her gorgeous green eyes!

Though her preferences seem to be shades of black and gray, Kristen can definitely pull off other colors beautifully! At the Rome premiere of *Twilight*, she looked refreshingly stunning in a bright white, fringed flapper dress. And at the Hollywood premiere of *Adventureland*, her amusement park coming-of-age comedy, she dazzled in a coral-colored backless Herve Leger dress with vertical black graphics.

When it comes to everyday makeup, Kristen prefers a more natural look over heavy color and definition. And with her pretty skin, killer cheekbones, and fine features, she doesn't need much makeup. A little mascara, a swipe of eyeliner, and some lip gloss, and she's ready to roll.

Dressed up or down, Kristen often wears her hair in a carelessly tousled way that matches her carefree attitude and down-to-earth style. When running around Hollywood, she'll either wear her hair down and loose, or she'll pull it all off her face and wear it back in a ponytail. On the red carpet, she wears it however the stylist does it—because she claims she would be completely incapable of styling her own hair!

In *Twilight*, Bella's style is somewhat similar to Kristen's in that they both dress so they're comfortable and not too noticeable. As Bella becomes more involved with Edward, she shifts to wearing cooler blues and grays as well as some romantic prints, like shirts with floral embroidery. This works well with her quiet personality and her warmer human character.

Kristen isn't particularly comfortable in front of the camera—unless, of course, she's in character and acting in a scene. Any photo shoots she does always involve a great deal of coaxing on the photographer's part to get some good poses.

In stark contrast to that is Ashley—a pro at posing thanks to her modeling background! Though she is similar to Kristen in that her preferred style is also casual—jeans, a shirt, and flats—she likes to add a bit of sass to her everyday outfits with accessories like a layered necklace and a slim biker jacket.

Ashley definitely enjoys all the opportunities she gets to play dress-up. When she does have to get glam for the cameras, she looks to Audrey Hepburn's classic, beautiful style as inspiration. At the *Twilight* premiere in Hollywood, Ashley wore her own stunning version of the Hepburn-inspired "little black dress"—a black bustier dress with a full ruffled skirt. A black and gold belt, black strappy Jimmy Choo shoes, and a black clutch purse finished off the look.

And at the 2009 MTV Movie Awards, instead of sporting something edgy or vampire-esque, Ashley took her look in an entirely different direction and rocked the look of a stylishly pretty pinup girl from the 1940s. She wore a form-fitting black-and-white flower print cocktail dress from Dolce & Gabbana with her hair fluffed up and out in pin curls. Purple pumps, a neon green clutch, and bright red lipstick completed the outfit—and brought her the distinction of being named by MTV as one of the Best Dressed Females at the annual awards show. Miley Cyrus, Sienna Miller, and Leighton Meester of *Gossip Girl* were also named on the list.

Ashley loves color—the bolder, the better! Whether she's rockin' candy apple red, deep purple, or sunflower yellow dresses; hanging out in a feminine fuchsia blouse with skinny jeans and heels; or a bright blue mini halter dress with sandals, she always looks picture-perfect.

When it comes to makeup, Ashley believes that less is more. She's not huge on foundation, but she always uses a little eyeliner, bronzer, and lip gloss. Even when she's dressed up, she goes for a more natural look, which totally enhances her charming girl-next-door beauty. The only aspect of her makeup that is regularly dramatic is her favorite bright red lipstick, which really pops against her creamy complexion.

Undoubtedly one of her best features, Ashley's lush, dark brown hair suits her dainty face. For *Twilight*, she wore a wig to capture Alice's pixie cut, and keeping her own thick hair under wraps proved to be quite a challenge for the stylists! So for *New Moon*, Ashley cut off several inches of her locks and, if it's even possible, looked even more adorable with a new chin-length 'do.

For Ashley, one of the absolute best parts of playing fashionista vampire Alice is the character's love of shopping and her huge wardrobe. "I got to merge modern day with the old style. It was very elegant and girlie," Ashley told mystyle.com.

Ashley's favorite fashion moment from *Twilight* was the first day of school, which is when the Cullens are first introduced. In the scene, Alice wears a flowing white shirt-dress with a black cropped vest and jeans. A black choker and chunky silver and turquoise bracelets complete the flirty but edgy costume. Ashley thought the whole outfit was just gorgeous.

Nikki's fashion style ranges from straight-up cool biker chick (just like BFF Kristen!) to flirty and feminine. She loves denim—skinny jeans, straight legs, cargo pants. She'll mix and match them with T-shirts, tank tops, cardigans, and jackets, and shoes like lace-up boots, sandals, and colorful sneakers. She likes to accessorize with rings, layered necklaces, scarves, and sometimes a funky hat. Some of her favorite stores for finding ultra-cool clothes include Fred Segal, Urban Outfitters, and Slow.

Nikki considers Audrey Hepburn and Merle Oberon, a British actress best known for her portrayal of Catherine in the film adapation of *Wuthering Heights* in 1939, as the most stylish women of all time in Hollywood. Looks like she chose the right people to style herself after! Even though she's still so young, Nikki's developed quite a signature style herself.

When it's time for her to hit the red carpet or other Hollywood event, Nikki is likely to choose a simple cocktail dress with little feminine touches, like a plunging neckline, petite bows on the shoulders, or a scalloped hemline. For the *Twilight* premiere,

Nikki shimmered in a black-and-white beaded Marchesa dress with black pumps. Her hair hung in loose curls with one side pulled up in a braid, revealing dangling orb earrings. With makeup in earth tones and bronzes accenting her dark features, she looked as warm and gorgeous as Rosalie is icy cool and beautiful.

With her long chestnut locks, Nikki enjoys wearing her hair in lots of different styles. When she wants to show off a dress, she'll often wear her hair in a sophisticated updo with some loose pieces softly framing her face. If she's out and about in Los Angeles, she may pull it off her face and into a ponytail, or even tuck it under a hat.

When it comes to fashion both on and off the red carpet, the lovely ladies of *Twilight* definitely know how to sparkle!

CHAPTER 18

Bites and Pieces

Kristen Stewart

Birthdate: April 9, 1990

Hometown: Woodland Hills, California

Hair color: Brown

Eye color: Green

Hobbies: Playing guitar, reading

Favorite music artists: Radiohead, The Beatles, The Specials, Laura Marling, Beck

Best music to dance with Rob Pattinson to: Iron and Wine, Van Morrison

Big names she's worked with: Jodie Foster, Robert DeNiro, Glenn Close

Actresses she'd like to work with: Evan Rachel Wood, Natalie Portman

Directors she'd like to work with: Martin Scorsese, Jodie Foster

Favorite book: *East of Eden* by John Steinbeck

Favorite authors: John Steinbeck, Albert Camus, Kurt Vonnegut

Favorite movie: *The Jungle Book* (She loves Disney movies!)

Movie she wishes she could have been in: *The Jungle Book* (as the voice of Mowgli)

Something you didn't know: Took swing dance lessons at Arthur Murray Dance Studio

Ashley Greene

Birthdate: February 21, 1987

Hometown: Jacksonville, Florida

Shares birthdate with: Ellen Page of *Juno* fame

Hair color: Dark brown

Eye color: Dark brown

Nicknames: Asher, Chewy (Bear)

Sibling: Older brother, Joe

Celebrity crushes: Christian Bale, Johnny Depp, Jon Hamm

Fashion icon: Audrey Hepburn

Favorite actors of all time: Audrey Hepburn, Meryl Streep, Charlize Theron, Rachel McAdams, Johnny Depp

Favorite TV show: *Mad Men*

Favorite music artists: Linkin Park, Muse, Paramore

Favorite dance music: Anything by Lil' Wayne

Favorite way to hang with friends: Hosting game nights with good friend Kellan Lutz, complete with Taboo and hors d'oeuvres

Pet: Dog, Marlow

Nikki Reed

Birthdate: May 17, 1988

Hometown: Los Angeles, California

Siblings: Two brothers, one older and one younger

Hair color: Dark brown

Eye color: Dark brown

Celebrity crushes: Val Kilmer in *Tombstone*, Paul Newman in *The Left Handed Gun*, Gary Oldman in *Basquiat*

Favorite movies: *City of God, True Romance, Nowhere in Africa, The Shawshank Redemption, The Lion King*

Favorite books: *Wuthering Heights, The Color of Water, Reading Lolita in Tehran, They Poured Fire on Us from the Sky, The Robber Bride, A Thousand Splendid Suns, Go Ask Alice, Schindler's List*

Favorite music artists: The Raconteurs and
 Kings of Leon

Hobbies: Reading, writing, horseback riding

Anna Kendrick

Birthdate: August 9, 1985

Hometown: Portland, Maine

Sibling: Older brother, Michael

Hair color: Medium brown

Eye color: Blue

Favorite treat: Banana dipped in chocolate
 wrapped in a pancake covered in
 banana-flavored whipped cream
 (from a chain of Japanese
 convenience stores in California)

Favorite color: Blue

Team Edward or Team Jacob: Team Jacob

Quote: "An actor should always let humility outweigh ambition."

Inspired by: Fearless women in comedy like Parker Posey, Molly Shannon, and Amy Poehler

If she had to go into hiding, she'd take: The entire Criterion DVD collection, a device for playing it, and a nap spa robe from Brookstone

Christian Serratos

Birthdate: September 21, 1990

Hometown: Pasadena, California

Hair color: Dark brown

Eye color: Dark brown

Nickname: Kish

Pets: A dog named Gorilla

Something you didn't know about her:

She's a vegetarian.

Favorite music artist: Paramore

Team Edward or Team Jacob: Team Edward

Favorite actors: James Spader, Johnny Depp, Adam Brody, Leonardo DiCaprio

Favorite actresses: Parker Posey, Jennifer Aniston, Sandra Bullock, Courtney Cox, Angelina Jolie

Favorite movie: *The House of Yes* (starring Parker Posey)

Three things she'd want if stuck on a deserted island: Portable Taco Bell, a radio, and her puppy

Other languages: Spanish (fluent)

Heritage: Italian, Mexican, and Irish

CHAPTER 19

Supernatural Girls Quiz

So how well do you know the leading ladies of *Twilight*? It's time to sink your teeth into a pop quiz! Good luck—and no peeking back to find the answers!

1) Which of the girls would be most familiar to Nickelodeon and Disney Channel audiences?

  A. Kristen Stewart

  B. Ashley Greene

  C. Nikki Reed

  D. Anna Kendrick

  E. Christian Serratos

2) Which of the girls auditioned for one of her roles by playing the guitar and singing the Beatles' song "Blackbird"?

   A. Kristen Stewart

   B. Ashley Greene

   C. Nikki Reed

   D. Anna Kendrick

   E. Christian Serratos

3) Which of the girls wrote a screenplay at a very young age?

   A. Kristen Stewart

   B. Ashley Greene

   C. Nikki Reed

   D. Anna Kendrick

   E. Christian Serratos

4) Which of the girls has a musical theater background?

    A. Kristen Stewart

    B. Ashley Greene

    C. Nikki Reed

    D. Anna Kendrick

    E. Christian Serratos

5) Which of the girls appeared on the MTV show *Punk'd* early on in her career?

    A. Kristen Stewart

    B. Ashley Greene

    C. Nikki Reed

    D. Anna Kendrick

    E. Christian Serratos

6) Which of the girls was born in Portland, Maine?

A. Kristen Stewart

B. Ashley Greene

C. Nikki Reed

D. Anna Kendrick

E. Christian Serratos

7) Which of the girls was born in Jacksonville, Florida?

A. Kristen Stewart

B. Ashley Greene

C. Nikki Reed

D. Anna Kendrick

E. Christian Serratos

8) Which of the girls has two parents and a brother in show business?

A. Kristen Stewart

B. Ashley Greene

C. Nikki Reed

D. Anna Kendrick

E. Christian Serratos

9) Which of the girls was a competitive figure skater?

A. Kristen Stewart

B. Ashley Greene

C. Nikki Reed

D. Anna Kendrick

E. Christian Serratos

10) Which of the girls was emancipated from her parents at the age of fourteen?

A. Kristen Stewart

B. Ashley Greene

C. Nikki Reed

D. Anna Kendrick

E. Christian Serratos

11) Which of the girls followed up *Twilight* with a role in a George Clooney film?

  A. Kristen Stewart

  B. Ashley Greene

  C. Nikki Reed

  D. Anna Kendrick

  E. Christian Serratos

12) Which of the girls wanted to be model at first, but was told she wasn't tall enough?

  A. Kristen Stewart

  B. Ashley Greene

  C. Nikki Reed

  D. Anna Kendrick

  E. Christian Serratos

13) Which of the girls plans to launch a clothing and jewelry line in the near future?

  A. Kristen Stewart

  B. Ashley Greene

C. Nikki Reed

D. Anna Kendrick

E. Christian Serratos

14) Which of the girls loves sneakers, especially her Converse?

    A. Kristen Stewart

    B. Ashley Greene

    C. Nikki Reed

    D. Anna Kendrick

    E. Christian Serratos

15) Which of the girls would like to direct films someday?

    A. Kristen Stewart

    B. Ashley Greene

    C. Nikki Reed

    D. Anna Kendrick

    E. Christian Serratos

16) Which of the girls won a Young Artist Award for her performance in *Twilight*?

    A. Kristen Stewart

    B. Ashley Greene

    C. Nikki Reed

    D. Anna Kendrick

    E. Christian Serratos

17) Which of the girls moved to Hollywood when she was just seventeen years old?

    A. Kristen Stewart

    B. Ashley Greene

    C. Nikki Reed

    D. Anna Kendrick

    E. Christian Serratos

18) Which of the girls was the second youngest actress to be nominated for a Tony Award?

A. Kristen Stewart

B. Ashley Greene

C. Nikki Reed

D. Anna Kendrick

E. Christian Serratos

19) Which of the girls likes horseback riding?

A. Kristen Stewart

B. Ashley Greene

C. Nikki Reed

D. Anna Kendrick

E. Christian Serratos

20) Which of the girls is a reader of classic literature and names *East of Eden* as her favorite book?

   A. Kristen Stewart

   B. Ashley Greene

   C. Nikki Reed

   D. Anna Kendrick

   E. Christian Serratos

CHAPTER 20
Supernatural Girls Online

With *New Moon* on the horizon, and two more amazing movies to follow, the careers and lives of the leading ladies are moving as fast as a speeding vampire! But here's the good news: You can always keep up with them online—either at official websites or at fansites.

Surfing the Internet for information on your favorite celebs—like Kristen, Ashley, Nikki, Anna, and Christian—is a lot of fun . . . but you have to be smart and safe about it.

First of all, you should only surf the Internet if you have your parents' permission. Never give out personal information—like your name, address, phone number, or even the name of your school or sports team. And it's very important that you don't ever try to meet someone in person who you met online.

Downloading pictures or other information from unknown sources is also not a good idea. In fact, if you're not sure whether or not to do something online, it's always just best to ask your parents. After all, there's not a butt-kicking vampire with superpowers around to help you!

Also remember that while there's a ton of information on celebrities on the Web, not all of it is necessarily true. Lots of people are creating websites out there, and sometimes they create false information to make their sites more exciting. Some people even pretend to be famous people online. So the best thing to do is go ahead and read all you want about your favorite *Twilight* stars—just remember that all of it might not be true!

Can't find your favorite website? That's the funny thing about websites—they tend to come and go. But don't worry—chances are there will be another one to replace it soon, especially with all the enthusiastic *Twilight* fans out there! After all, the more *Twilight*, the better!

Sites about the Twilight Saga

There are tons of *Twilight*-related sites on the Internet. Both of the official websites listed below contain links to many, many other *Twilight* sites that you can check out on your own!

www.twilightthemovie.com

The official website for the *Twilight* movies. Exclusive content about *New Moon* and *Twilight* can be found here.

www.stepheniemeyer.com

The official website of Stephenie Meyer, author of the *Twilight* series.

www.twilightlexicon.com

An excellent fansite for the Twilight saga that includes, among other great information, personal correspondence between the site's founder and Stephenie Meyer that shares lots of background information on the books' characters and Stephenie's vampire world.

www.twilighters.org

A great fansite for those *Twilight* addicts interested in up-to-the-minute news and photos about the Twilight saga and any of the actors from the movies. It also includes information about the books and movies, plus lots of extras.

www.bellaandedward.com

A fantastic fansite with the latest information on all things *Twilight,* including photos, video clips, and news.

Sites about the Girls

There are lots of fansites dedicated to *Twilight*'s leading ladies. Here are some good ones.

Kristen
www.kstewartfan.org
www.kristenstewartdaily.net

Nikki
www.nikkireedfan.com
www.nicolereed.org

Ashley
www.ashleygreene.net
www.ashley-greene.com

Anna
www.annakendrickonline.org

Christian
www.christian-serratos.org